Treating the Neurotic Patient in Brief Psychotherapy

Edited by
Althea J. Horner

JASON ARONSON INC.
Northvale, New Jersey
London

THE MASTER WORK SERIES

First softcover edition 1994

Copyright © 1994, 1985 by Jason Aronson Inc.

Library of Congress Cataloging-in-Publication Data *pending*

ISBN: 1-56821-212-7

Manufactured in the United States of America. Jason Aronson Inc. offers books and cassettes. For information and catalog write to Jason Aronson Inc., 230 Livingston Street, Northvale, New Jersey 07647.

CONTRIBUTORS

Harold Been, M.D.
Physician-in-Charge
Center for Teaching and Research in
   Short-Term Dynamic Psychotherapy
Department of Psychiatry
Beth Israel Medical Center

Senior Clinical Instructor
Mount Sinai School of Medicine
City University of New York

Walter Flegenheimer, M.D.
Associate Attending
Center for Teaching and Research in
   Short-Term Dynamic Psychotherapy
Department of Psychiatry
Beth Israel Medical Center

Assistant Clinical Professor of Psychiatry
Mount Sinai School of Medicine
City University of New York

Victor Goldin, M.D.
Associate Director for Education

Department of Psychiatry
Beth Israel Medical Center

Assistant Professor of Clinical Psychiatry
Mount Sinai School of Medicine
City University of New York

Althea J. Horner, Ph.D.
Senior Faculty, Wright Institute Los Angeles Postgraduate Center
Clinical Professor, Department of Psychology, U.C.L.A.

Associate Clinical Professor of Psychiatry
Mount Sinai School of Medicine
City University of New York

Isabel Sklar, M.S.W.
Associate Director
Department of Social Work
Beth Israel Medical Center

Teaching Associate
Departments of Psychiatry and Community Medicine
Mount Sinai School of Medicine
City University of New York

Manuel Trujillo, M.D.
Physician-in-Charge
Research and Program Evaluation
Department of Psychiatry
Beth Israel Medical Center

Assistant Professor of Clinical Psychiatry
Mount Sinai School of Medicine
City University of New York

Arnold Winston, M.D.
Director
Department of Psychiatry
Beth Israel Medical Center

Professor of Clinical Psychiatry
Mount Sinai School of Medicine
City University of New York

ACKNOWLEDGMENTS

The work described in this book has come out of the brief psychotherapy clinical and research project undertaken in 1979 by the Department of Psychiatry at Beth Israel Medical Center in New York City under the leadership of Dr. Arnold Winston, Director of the Department, in response to the growing interest in and the need for shorter treatment of the nonseriously ill patient. Both the Sifneos and Davanloo models were applied in the project as was another approach developed at Beth Israel under the co-leadership of myself and Jerome Pollack, M.D., to provide a comparison group within the research design. This approach has been named "brief adaptation-oriented psychotherapy" (BAP). The material on ego and superego evaluation (chapters 4 and 5) is from the BAP manual.

We, the writers of this book, wish to acknowledge the contributions made by everyone who participated in and continues to participate in the project: Barbara Mattacotta, former Department Administrator, who formulated, directed, and managed the formidable task of record-keeping and scheduling; Lorraine Friedman, present Department Administrator, who continued the direction and coordination of the project; Margaret M. Nepps, Psy.D., who helped develop the intake procedures and did the psychological testing; and

Lucia Vail, Ellen Kesller, Rachel Fishman, and Christine Wright who assisted with the evaluation and preliminary screening of patients. Their participation and input is gratefully acknowledged. Thanks are also due Marjorie Raskin, M.D., for her input in the early planning stages of the book.

CONTENTS

Need for Systematic Guidelines • Some Principles of Treatment •
The Use of Video Equipment in the Course of Treatment •
Supervision: An Integral Part of Therapy

INTRODUCTION

The purpose of this book is to offer the reader a particular expertise — that of conducting brief psychotherapy with the neurotic patient so that, as mental health professionals, readers may undertake
this challenging and rewarding method of treatment. The fact that
treatment is shorter does not mean that it is easier or less demand-
ing of the therapist. Quite the contrary. It demands a clarity of
thinking and precision of purpose that takes time and motivation
to develop. It is hoped by the several writers who have contributed
to this book that it will indeed be useful toward that end.

In short-term anxiety-provoking psychotherapy (STAPP) (Sifneos 1979), one finds that many of the patients who present themselves for brief treatment do not respond because of deeply entrenched
obsessive defenses or dependent passivity. Davanloo's *Short-Term
Dynamic Psychotherapy* (STDP) (1980) extends brief treatment to
a much wider selection of patients.

This book focuses on the Sifneos formulations as applied in
the clinical setting, with modified application of Davanloo's techniques in instances of more deeply entrenched characterological resistances.

It becomes clear that the various approaches share certain basic
tenets, the sine qua non of brief psychotherapy. These principles
are described in Chapter 1 by Flegenheimer in his overview of the

brief therapies. In the practice of brief treatment, as long as there is strict observance of these basic tenets, there is room for considerable variation of technique according to the presenting problem and the nature of the patient's defenses, as well as the personal predeliction of the therapist. Dr. Been describes the tailoring of approach on the basis of the absence or presence of certain characterological defenses.

In Chapter 1, Flegenheimer emphasizes (1) the establishment and maintenance of a treatment focus, (2) the activity of the therapist, and (3) the early and consistent interpretation of transference as a resistance and/or as it relates to the agreed upon focus.

Since all patients selected for brief treatment as described in this book show no significant preoedipal pathology (a selection criterion), the oedipal focus tends to leap forward readily with the men and women who present with problems in their work and in their interpersonal relationships. In Chapter 2 Horner lays out the steps required for the resolution of the Oedipus complex and provides a theoretical backdrop for this operationalized approach to treatment.

In Chapter 3, Goldin discusses in greater detail certain clinical issues such as (1) time and tempo, (2) focus maintenance, (3) transference and countertransference, and (4) intervention. He also emphasizes the need for appropriate supervision and review, telling us that no therapist, no matter how well trained, can undertake this work without spending extensive time and effort in perfecting the technique. It is paradoxical that the brevity of treatment, which is so beneficial to the patient, requires so much extra time and effort on the part of the therapist. Goldin describes the twin processes of supervision and self-supervision, which the independent practitioner can undertake.

In two chapters Horner outlines the mechanics of brief treatment, specifics of technique that apply to all forms of brief psychotherapy, some of which may well increase the efficacy of long-term treatment as well. These are activity, clarity, specificity, immediacy, interpreting upward, maintaining the focus, monitoring the transference, and the triads of interpretation.

Horner presents an ego psychological approach to evaluation for suitability for brief psychotherapy. The ego and superego functions to be evaluated are operationally defined. These include relation to reality, regulation and control of instinctual drives, object relations, thought processes, defenses, autonomous functions, the synthetic function, conscience, and the ego-ideal.

In Chapter 6 Been describes the clinical interview and the evaluation process, telling us that patients with simple, focused complaints related to oedipal material can be interviewed with little attention paid to characterological issues. On the other hand, patients with many characterological problems such as obsessional defenses, passivity, and dependency require much more immediate attention to characterological resistance in order to assess the patient's potential for affective responsiveness. These interviews use the techniques developed by Davanloo and have a flavor that is less cognitive and more confrontive.

Been goes on to describe how the therapist goes about evaluating ego assets of patients for short-term psychotherapy. These major necessary ego capacities are (1) the ability to form meaningful give-and-take relationships, (2) the ability to tolerate strong affects associated with anger, guilt, depression, and anxiety, (3) characterological flexibility, and (4) positive response to interpretation.

Been gives clinical examples of the assessment of the quality of interpersonal relationships and of the exploration of the psychodynamics and structure. Finally, he describes the setting of the contract with an agreement as to what the focus of the therapy will be.

In Chapter 7, Winston and Trujillo examine the uncovering process, defining its goals in accord with the steps necessary to the resolution of the Oedipus complex, which are delineated in Chapter 2. They write that the most important of these goals is the uncovering of the basic oedipal wishes, that is, the desire to defeat and displace the same-sex parent in order to have a primary and erotic relationship with the parent of the opposite sex.

They describe the fears related to the possible actualization of the wishes — "the loss of control that might allow incest, patricide, or matricide" — as well as the possible consequences of this eventuality. Winston and Trujillo also describe the necessity of uncovering the negative affects associated with the frustration of oedipal wishes — the anger and disappointment, the outrage and betrayal, the humiliation of defeat, and "the fear of being banished from the triangle for forbidden desires."

Winston and Trujillo narrate the technical aspects of uncovering and relate them to the specific requirements of brief treatment, giving clinical examples. They emphasize that the uncovering must go on at an experiential level and that one does not short-circuit the process by giving the patient an unexperienced cognitive view of his problems.

In the next chapter, Winston and Trujillo explore the working-through phase of the treatment process and again relate its goals to those set forth in Chapter 2.

They use Greenson's (1967) formulation of the working-through process — the complex set of procedures and processes that occurs after an insight has been given.

The goals of this phase of treatment include giving up the wish to have the opposite-sex parent sexually and/or to be the preferred object. In addition, identification with the opposite-sex parent must be acknowledged without the fear of loss of gender identity.

The wish to defeat in competition, displace, or to murder the same-sex parent must also be renounced, and identifications with that parent must be acknowledged without endangering the patient's ego-ideal. Again Winston and Trujillo illustrate with clinical examples.

The resolution phase of the treatment process is described in Chapter 9 by Trujillo and Winston, who note that the main task is to consolidate the gains of insight obtained in the earlier phases. Typically there is full acknowledgment of the oedipal wishes and a reformulation of the patient's real relationship to his or her parents. Often a more genuine acceptance of the parents' positive and negative aspects evolves along with the emergence, in these relationships, of previously unknown features such as intimacy, and a sense of personal closeness. Clinical vignettes illustrate the complexities of this phase of treatment.

In Chapter 10 Trujillo and Winston describe the termination phase of treatment, noting that patients with whom the transference has been thoroughly interpreted tend to accept termination readily and often bring it up themselves following a discussion of evidence of tangible change in their lives. Typically, the well-selected patient goes on working right up to the last session.

They note that in the presence of more complicated psychopathology, but still within the oedipal spectrum, termination may bring about a transitory recrudescence of symptoms. In these patients specific symptoms and defenses about termination have to be worked through. Trujillo and Winston note that the successful working through of loss issues requires detailed attention to the transferential implications.

The verbatim record of part of a single case is presented in Chapter 11 to illustrate the major principles of brief treatment: (1) the activity of the therapist, (2) the maintenance of the focus, and (3) the interpretation of transference resistances.

Sklar in Chapter 12 reports some of the outcomes of brief psychotherapy with oedipal patients.

With the consolidation of brief psychotherapy as a technique, we may begin to ask if it might not be applicable to a wider variety of presenting problems. In my supervision in private practice, I have found it useful for bringing to a close long-term therapies that have become bogged down because of the failure to address a central transference resistance, particularly the "overthrow" of the authority of the therapist. Setting a termination contract and applying the principles of brief psychotherapy enable the therapist to bring the treatment to a constructive close in contrast to the unresolved endings that take place in many such situations.

For those of us who have worked with this modality, there is no doubt of its almost startling efficacy in many situations. Creative use of its principles may show, over time, that it does indeed have wider applicability and that what we can learn from it will add to the effectiveness of long-term treatment and reduce the length of that therapy.

References

Davanloo, H. (1980). *Short-Term Dynamic Psychotherapy*. New York: Jason Aronson.

Greenson, R. (1967). *The Technique and Practice of Psychoanalysis*. New York: International Universities Press.

Sifneos, P. (1979). *Short-Term Dynamic Psychotherapy*. New York: Plenum Press.

Chapter 1

HISTORY OF BRIEF PSYCHOTHERAPY

WALTER FLEGENHEIMER, M.D.

The current interest in psychoanalytically oriented brief psychotherapy grew out of work that began in the late 1950s and early 1960s. In that period most training centers were treating a small number of patients with long-term psychoanalytically oriented psychotherapy. Because many people wanted treatment, long waiting lists of unserved patients were common. The techniques developed at that time were initially created as an expedient alternative to long-term therapy. It was soon noted, however, that these new techniques were not only helpful in reducing waiting lists and meeting the requirements of third-party payers, but they were also effective and could, in some cases, produce results comparable to those of long-term therapy. Some of these techniques have been refined and are still being used, and their early promise has been justified by the good results that are being achieved.

Certain factors characterize brief psychotherapy as it is used today and distinguish it from other forms of analytically oriented psychotherapy (Marmor 1979):

1. The criteria for selecting patients for brief psychotherapy are usually different from those of longer therapies.
2. It is understood by both patient and therapist that the therapy will be brief (the usual range is from 12–40 sessions).
3. The therapist is more active than in other therapies.

4. The emotional tension of the therapy is maintained at a rather high level throughout the treatment.
5. The patient's material is focused on certain issues to the exclusion of others.
6. Early transference interpretations are common.

Although all the above factors have been brought together in a systematic manner only within the past 20 years, important aspects of today's brief therapy techniques can be traced to the earliest days of psychoanalysis, that is, to Breuer and Freud's (1895) *Studies on Hysteria*. Thereafter the development of brief psychotherapy and the development of psychoanalysis were intertwined in such a way that most major attempts at promoting brief psychotherapy were seen by Freud and his followers as attempts to modify and undermine the basic principles of psychoanalysis and thus to destroy psychoanalysis as they understood it (Flegenheimer 1982).

Freud

In *Studies on Hysteria*, Breuer and Freud postulated that symptoms were caused by the repression of traumatic memories and their accompanying affects. If these memories could be brought into consciousness and the affects experienced and discharged, the symptoms would abate. The aim of their treatment was to get the patient to remember the traumatic event that first led to the formation of symptoms. In the original patient treated by Breuer, Anna O., Breuer used hypnosis to allow the patient to overcome her resistances and remember the origins of her various symptoms. In later cases, all treated by Freud, hypnosis was used at times. However, Freud, noting that all patients could not be hypnotized, developed his "concentration" technique, which consisted of the patient lying on a couch with eyes closed and Freud applying pressure on the forehead from time to time to help the patient concentrate on trying to remember the events surrounding the origin of the symptom. By means of the patient's efforts and the therapist's urgings, the lost memories and affects were recovered. Later Freud stopped applying pressure to the forehead and urged the patient to remember without any physical contact.

Although the treatments described in *Studies on Hysteria* differ in many ways from current techniques of brief psychotherapy, common elements can be found in the two modes of treatment. Thus, though Freud did not describe any formal selection criteria for his patients, what he wrote about the characteristics of patients suited for his treatment anticipates, to some extent, current selection requirements for brief psychotherapy. Freud is clear that the cathartic method is not suitable for every patient. He states that the patient must have a "certain level of intelligence." He must have confidence in the procedure; that is, the patient must begin the treatment with a positive attitude toward the therapist and his particular mode of therapy and the patient must show a high level of motivation so that he can overcome the resistance that will be aroused when the patient sees "the direction in which the treatment is going," i.e., the sexual origins of the neurosis (Chapter 4). In contrast to brief psychotherapies today, Freud did not select patients on the basis of their psychological health. Indeed, most of Freud's early patients were severely ill people who had proven refractory to other forms of treatment and had come to Freud after other physicians had failed to provide relief of their symptoms. For the same reason, Freud did not select patients on the basis of the focality of their symptoms.

Of the cases described in *Studies on Hysteria*, only Lucy R. fits into the time frame that today constitutes brief psychotherapy. She was seen approximately once a week for nine weeks, but no infantile traumata were involved in the clearing of her symptoms. Katerina was seen by Freud on only one occasion. The other patients were seen usually in daily visits: Emmy Von N. for seven weeks during her first year of treatment and for eight weeks in her second year of treatment, Anna O. for about 18 months, and no time of treatment is given for Elisabeth Von R., although the treatment was not brief. Freud was developing a new technique for treating serious conditions that heretofore had resisted all available treatment modalities, and he was not concerned with the problems of how long the therapy would last. Although these early patients were not aware that their therapy was supposed to be "brief," neither did they have the expectation, so common today, that psychotherapy is of necessity a lengthy process. Thus the open-ended, timeless quality, so characteristic of much of current therapy, was not a factor at that time.

Freud advocates a great deal of activity for the therapist. The therapist must have confidence in his technique and he must convey this to the patient. The therapist frequently "insists" that the patient can produce a thought or a memory relevant to the topic being explored. He uses pressure on the forehead of the patient to encourage the flow of the material. When there is resistance, the therapist will often attack it directly. One of the few examples that quotes Freud and the patient extensively in *Studies on Hysteria* (p. 113) clearly illustrates these points. The therapist speaks as often and as extensively as the patient. Freud is as persistent and "relentless" in overcoming the patient's resistances and maintaining the focus as Sifneos and Davanloo are today. In addition to confronting the patient and insisting that the patient can produce relevant material, the therapist is also supportive and educational, informing the patient of the workings of the mind and getting the patient to participate in the treatment as a "collaborator," thus undoing some of the dependency incurred by the authoritative stance of the therapist.

Although a focus as such is not mentioned in *Studies on Hysteria*, the technique consisted of following only those ideas that occurred to the patient in relation to each symptom. Each symptom was thus "analyzed" until its traumatic origins were elucidated and the appropriate affect experienced. By concentrating on the connections to a specific symptom, other thoughts were excluded, and the effect was to limit the treatment to a circumscribed set of associations. No characterological issues were dealt with. Little attention was paid to what was later called "working through" or to issues of termination.

In *Studies on Hysteria*, Freud is already aware of the concept of transference and states that transference can be utilized in the treatment, although he does not emphasize this aspect of the treatment. Indeed, he states that material may be considered *either* in the transference or in the memories of past events:

> "For the patient the work remained the same: she had to overcome the distressing affect aroused by having been able to entertain such a wish even for a moment; and it seemed to make no difference to the success of the treatment whether she made this psychical repudiation the theme of her work in the historical instance or in the recent one connected with me" (p. 304).

It is only later that the transference becomes the essential element in the therapy.

Freud soon repudiated his cathartic method. In "Dora" (*A Case of Hysteria* 1905, p. 12) he writes that since *Studies on Hysteria*, "psycho-analytic technique has been completely revolutionized." He then describes the new technique of free association, stating that it is much superior to the older one, which followed the associations back from the symptoms; "indeed there can be no doubt that it [i.e., the new technique] can be *the only possible one*" [italics added]. Freud's statement lays the foundation for the subsequent resistance to brief psychotherapy. Freud, in trying to develop psychoanalysis, discarded his cathartic technique and never pursued it to fully determine its usefulness or limitations. He was not interested in forms of psychotherapy other than psychoanalysis, and, indeed, he saw any deviation from psychoanalysis as a threat to psychoanalysis itself. As psychoanalysis developed, therapy took longer and longer and was less and less similar to brief psychotherapy as we know it today. The activity of the therapist declined; he became less challenging and supportive; and the use of free associations eliminated the focusing of treatment on only one aspect of the patient's mental productions.

These changes followed inevitably from the technique of free association. An active therapist is incompatible with a free-associating patient. The more the therapist talks, the more he interrupts the patient's associations so that Freud's "new technique" led to the increasing inactivity and passivity of the therapist. The combination of the patient's free association and the passive therapist resulted in a deepening regression leading to the formation of the transference neurosis, which, of course, required time to analyze once it was formed. Once it was recognized that the transference neurosis was the main therapeutic tool, those factors that tended to help form the transference neurosis were, of course, encouraged.

Although Freud (1905) advocated the technique of free association in "Dora," it can be seen from the case material that Freud was still an extremely active therapist, especially when his technique is compared with today's typical analytic technique. Gill (1982) recently reviewed the available literature on what Freud actually did during his therapy sessions in contrast to what he wrote on the subject of therapeutic technique. The only sources that can be used are Freud's case histories and the published memoirs of those who were analyzed by Freud. Although recognizing that the data are very sparse, Gill believes that the evidence clearly shows that Freud remained active throughout his career despite what he wrote and what his followers practiced.

Malan (1963) reviewed "analytic" cases that were published by therapists other than Freud before 1914. These treatments were often relatively brief and successful. He notes that many of these therapies still followed the cathartic method. A review of his sources reveals a varying mixture of cathartic and analytic techniques that were being carried on long after Freud had abandoned all elements of the cathartic method in his own work. The work of these early therapists is characterized by the kind of drama and enthusiasm that is seen in much of today's brief therapy. In addition, there was much attention paid to "complexes," which were groups of associations, memories, and affects organized around a particular traumatic event, usually in childhood. The aim of the therapy was often to follow the associations of the complex until all aspects of the complex could be made conscious. By concentrating on the analysis of the complexes, these early therapists were practicing focal therapy, although that term was not used by the writers of that time. The early case material that was published is limited, and it is not clear how much of this type of therapy was actually being practiced between 1895 and 1914. There is much anecdotal material about the early brief and successful therapies, but little hard data. What is clear is that this type of case material ceases to appear in the analytic literature after 1914.

Freud himself conducted therapies that were brief in time, but his brief treatments were different from the early cathartic therapies and from brief therapy as it is known today. He treated Bruno Walter successfully for cramps in his conducting arm in a few visits in 1906, but the therapy consisted of a suggestion to take a vacation. When the symptom was still present on Walter's return, Freud told him that he would gradually be able to conduct, and these later suggestions did, indeed, work (Sterba 1951). How many brief suggestive treatments Freud engaged in is not known, because he never published any of them. The Bruno Walter therapy came to light only because Walter published it in his memoirs. Freud's training analyses were often brief, the early ones sometimes lasting only a few weeks, but Freud distinguished between training analyses and therapeutic analyses. It is not known how many "brief" therapeutic analyses Freud conducted.

Ferenczi and Rank

Ferenczi and Rank (1925) were the first major writers to address the issue of the increasing duration of psychoanalytic treatments. Their book, *The Development of Psychoanalysis*, was written in 1922, published in German in 1923, and in English translation in 1925. The book is a difficult one to read. The language used is quite out of date and no case examples are given to clarify the points made. In addition, the authors were probably trying to be circumspect in presenting their ideas so as not to run counter to the main tenets of psychoanalysis. Despite this, it is possible to see in this work important precursors of present day brief psychotherapy.

Rank was the first to advocate using a fixed time limit for most patients in psychoanalysis. [Freud (1937) used a fixed time limit with the "Wolfman" and other cases, but he never advocated the general application of this technique.] Rank set a time limit for treatment after the transference neurosis was formed. He believed that in the beginning of the treatment, when there was no time limit, the patient's early childhood fantasies were mobilized and gratified within the transference. He thought that a time limit was necessary for the patient to be able to confront reality and learn to give up the unrealistic aspects of these fantasies. The use of a time limit as a concretization of reality anticipates the work of Mann. (See below.)

Whereas Rank is associated with the development of the time limit, Ferenczi (1952) is known for advocating "active" therapy. In a series of papers dating from 1919 to 1925, Ferenczi noted that there were limitations to the technique of free association and that at times specific commands should be given to the patient, either to engage in, or to desist from, certain activities. He emphasized that these active techniques are the exception to the rule of free association and should be used rarely and only when clearly indicated, for example, with a severe obsessional patient as a means of combating the patient's intellectualizing. In taking this position, he did not differ significantly from positions taken by Freud.

In *The Development of Psychoanalysis*, however, Ferenczi and Rank describe a much broader role for the active therapist than was given in the above cited papers. They note that psychoanalysis often becomes overly intellectual. They believe that this is often a result of mixing up the investigative and therapeutic aspects of psychoanalysis. As a research tool, psychoanalysis is an indispensible technique for exploring the development of the mind, but often analysts, in their desire to corroborate their theory with each patient, undertake a complete analysis when this is not really necessary. Ferenczi and Rank emphasize that "in the correctly executed analysis the whole development of the individual is not repeated, but only those phases of development of the infantile libido on which the ego . . . has remained fixed" (p. 19). When the therapy goes deeper than is necessary, treatment becomes too intellectual for the patient because he no longer is that emotionally invested in the problems that arise. Intellectual knowledge without affect serves as a resistance. The therapist, therefore, must be active to maintain the therapy at the proper level and to avoid associations that go beyond this level. (This is related to maintaining a focus.) The therapist must also be active to maintain the proper emotional tension throughout the treatment.

Ferenczi and Rank state that change comes about through the patient's experiencing the affects as well as the intellectual understanding of his original, usually oedipal, conflict in the transference. To evoke the necessary affect, which they say is achieved with the cathartic method but which is often not experienced through free associations alone, the therapist must at times be active, in order to "provoke" the affects, either by direct commands or prohibitions, or by assuming a transference stance that is fitted to the needs of the patient and that will elicit the desired affect. [Here they anticipate Alexander's "manipulation" of the transference (see below).]

Thus, one can see in *The Development of Psychoanalysis* three of the main elements of brief psychotherapy, albeit in rough form — the time limit, the focus, and the active therapist keeping the emotional tension high. Why this material was generally ignored for 20 years until reformulated by Alexander (1946) is a complicated story involving, amont other things, the personalities of Ferenczi and Rank and their personal relationship with Freud and his close associates, as well as Freud's need to maintain the integrity of the psychoanalytic movement (Jones 1957).

At that time, psychoanalysis was the only accepted form of psychoanalytically oriented psychotherapy, so that there was no precedence for introducing alternative forms of treatment within the psychoanalytic movement. But, in fact, Ferenczi and Rank did not present their proposals as *alternatives* to psychoanalysis suitable for certain patients, but rather they saw their modifications of technique as a general *substitute* for psychoanalysis. It can easily be seen, therefore, that Freud and his other followers would experience *The Development of Psychoanalysis* as a direct attack on their own work. During this period Rank's ideas about therapy became connected with his theory that the birth trauma was the central issue in neurosis and that this was all that had to be analyzed. This concept, combined with the time limit, resulted in quite short treatments, often only three to four months long. In rejecting the Oedipus complex as central to the genesis of the neurosis, Rank took a position that Freud could not accept, and the two men broke their relationship in 1926. Most of Ferenczi's contributions to brief therapy were also lost in controversy. During the late 1920s he became increasingly estranged from Freud, although they never terminated their friendship. His active therapy, which was originally quite conservative, became more and more extreme, leading to physical contact between himself and his patients and to other attempts by him to directly gratify some of the patient's previously unsatisfied needs. By the time of his death in 1933 Ferenczi had lost much of the influence he had previously had in the psychoanalytic community.

Alexander

Between the appearance of Ferenczi and Rank's book in 1923 and Alexander and French's book in 1946, little was published in the psychiatric literature on the subject of brief psychotherapy, and what there was tended to be anecdotal and undocumented. In 1938 Franz Alexander, then head of the Chicago Institute for Psychoanalysis, began a research project to "define those basic principles which make possible a shorter and more efficient means of psychotherapy, and whenever possible to develop specific means of treatment" (1946, p. iii). As part of this project, members of the Chicago Institute treated nearly 600 patients at both the Institute and in private practice. The result of their work was published by Alexander and French in their book *Psychoanalytic Therapy*.

Alexander's work is a direct continuation of the work of Ferenczi and Rank's, as Alexander readily acknowledges. However, in contrast to Ferenczi and Rank, Alexander presents his ideas in a clear and forceful manner, well documented with case material. He held a prestigious position in the psychoanalytic community and was able to bring his prestige and that of his Institute to bear on the question of modifying psychoanalysis.

Alexander began by questioning the assumptions that had governed Freud and his followers: that depth of therapy and quality of therapeutic results are *necessarily* proportionate to length of treatment and to the frequency of the interviews. Once these assumptions are questioned, the development of alternative, briefer techniques becomes possible. In certain circumstances these new techniques may be as efficacious as classical analysis. Indeed, Alexander goes further and states that some of the alternative techniques may often be superior to psychoanalysis in that psychoanalysis often perpetuates the patient's regression. The gratification the patient receives from the regression, and hence from the treatment, may lead not only to unnecessarily prolonged treatments, but also to treatments that end unsuccessfully.

Much of what Alexander advocates is designed to minimize regression. Like Ferenczi and Rank, he believes that it is not necessary to analyze all aspects of every patient's mental life. Analysis need only go back to the point at which the trauma that caused the present difficulty occurred. Any probing beyond (i.e., developmentally earlier) that point is not therapeutic and only leads to nonproductive regression. Such technical devices as using weekly sessions, varying the frequency of the sessions, interrupting the treatment, and using the chair instead of the couch are used to help minimize the regression.

Each patient, after an initial evaluation, should have a specific individual treatment plan devised on the basis of as complete a psychodynamic understanding of the patient as is possible. Included in the evaluation are not only such factors as the developmental phase to which the symptoms can be traced and the type of resistances that the patient shows, but also the ego strengths of the patient. The stronger the patient's ego, the more will the therapist push the material, resulting in a more intense and briefer therapy (this anticipates Sifneos 1979 — see below). Although some of the cases described by Alexander are quite brief, he does not set a time limit, nor does he tell the patient that the therapy will be a brief one.

The therapist is very active in order to minimize regression and to keep the emotional tension high throughout the treatment. Like Ferenczi and Rank, Alexander believes in the importance of the emotional component of the therapy. Indeed, he believes that what he calls the "corrective emotional experience" is essential to affecting change in any treatment. The corrective emotional experience is the reliving by the patient of the original traumatic experience in relation to the therapist or to some other person in his life, this time with a more favorable resolution than in the original childhood conflict. By recognizing that the corrective emotional experience can occur either inside or outside the transference to the therapist, Alexander eliminates the necessity of having the transference be the central focus in every treatment situation. He returns here to ideas first formulated by Freud in *Studies on Hysteria*. Alexander advocates that the therapist "manipulate" the transference, that is, assume a role that will most readily evoke the corrective emotional experience.

Today, many of Alexander's ideas seem commonplace, because so many of them have been adopted by therapists practicing analytically oriented psychotherapy, but at the time his contributions were quite controversial. There are two main reasons for the controversy. First, some aspects of his technique have never been generally accepted. His ideas about trial interruptions of treatment and manipulation of transference have not been widely adopted. His theory of the corrective emotional experience is also generally not given the central place in the theory of change that it had for Alexander. The second main source of controversy was a result of Alexander's method of presenting his ideas. Again, as with Ferenczi and Rank, the distinction between psychotherapy and psychoanalysis became blurred. By 1946 psychoanalysis and analytically oriented psychotherapy were generally understood to be two separate, if related, modalities of treatment. Alexander is well aware of the distinction and refers to the classical analytic technique as "the standard technique." He sees the "standard technique" as one variant of psycho-analytic therapy. Although Alexander acknowledges that the "standard technique" might be useful for chronic neurosis, his general tone throughout the book is one of condescension for an inferior method of treatment and quite similar in tone to that used by Freud and his followers when discussing therapies other than psychoanalysis. Thus, many critics responded to Alexander's attacks on psychoanalysis, rather than focusing on the substance of his work. Once again, the main issue became one of defending Freud and classical psychoanalysis against any encroachment, and in this process many valuable contributions of Alexander were generally overlooked. Interestingly, Alexander influenced long-term analytically oriented psychotherapy almost immediately, but he had little influence on brief therapy for nearly 20 years, even though his case material contains many brief cases and much of what he wrote has direct application to brief therapy techniques. It is not clear why this should be so. Probably the jump from psychoanalysis to brief therapy was too great a leap, and it was necessary for analytically oriented long-term therapy to be established as a legitimate and effective modality of treatment before further modifications could be entertained by the profession.

Malan

A hiatus in the brief psychotherapy literature occurred after Alexander's book, similar to the one that had preceded it. Although isolated reports were published, nothing of a systematic nature appeared until the publication of David Malan's *A Study of Brief Psychotherapy* in 1963. Malan's work grew out of a workshop started by Michael Balint at the Tavistock clinic in London in 1955. This workshop, led by Malan after Balint's death, not only produced two research studies in brief psychotherapy but also developed the technique of brief psychotherapy that is now associated with Malan's name (Malan, 1976a, 1976b). The details of the research will not be considered here other than to note that the data clearly show that patients can achieve long-lasting psychodynamic and characterological changes through the application of these brief techniques.

Malan is not as specific as some of the other recent workers in defining his selection criteria and technique of therapy. After an extensive initial evaluation, if the patient is selected for brief psychotherapy, a time limit of 20 to 30 sessions is set, the length depending on the experience of the therapist and the severity of the problem. A history of serious psychopathology excludes the patient. It is necessary that the evaluator find a focus that is meaningful dynamically as well as in terms of the current symptoms. The focus can be either oedipal or one dealing with loss. Most important is the patient's ability to respond to a trial interpretation during the evaluation interview. In addition, the patient must show an ability to relate to the examiner and must have an adequate degree of motivation, though this is not defined.

Malan also uses the standard techniques of analytically oriented psychotherapy, interpreting resistances and defenses before the impulses and wishes are clarified. He emphasizes the importance of the therapist-parent link, that is, being able to show the patient the conflict in the transference and then relating it to his past life. Although Malan is careful to keep the patient within the focus, his technique is not particularly confronting or harsh. In recent years Malan has advocated the use of the technique of Davanloo (1980). Malan believes that it is more efficacious and has wider applicability than the technique he himself described. Nevertheless, others have continued using and building on the technique that Malan developed and then abandoned. The work of Marmor (1979) and the "brief adaptational psychotherapy" currently being developed at the Beth Israel Medical Center in New York are examples of currently used techniques that grew out of the work of Malan.

Sifneos

In 1956 Peter Sifneos successfully treated a 28-year-old man suffering from severe anxiety that centered on the patient's upcoming marriage. Seven weeks were available between the time the patient came to Sifneos and the wedding, and so the treatment lasted seven weeks. Following this experience, Sifneos (1972, 1979) began a systematic study of what was possible with short-term therapy and subsequently developed the technique he calls short-term anxiety-provoking psychotherapy (STAPP). Sifneos' technique follows the principle stated by Alexander: the stronger the patient's ego, the more can the therapist push the material. Sifneos picks very healthy patients and pushes them very hard.

Sifneos is very careful to delineate specific criteria for selecting patients. A patient suitable for STAPP is a basically healthy person who has demonstrated his or her ability to function in both vocational and personal areas of life. The patient must have a delimited chief complaint, must be psychologically minded, and must be well motivated to work in treatment. The patient should have a circumscribed area of complaint, and the therapist must be able to understand the underlying dynamics of the symptoms. The symptoms (whether appearing as isolated symptoms or as manifestations of interpersonal or characterological problems) should be derivatives of an oedipal conflict. Although patients meeting these criteria do exist, they tend to be rare at most mental health facilities, and, indeed, the strictness of the selection criteria has been a key factor in limiting the general usefulness of this technique.

The hallmark of this technique is the activity of the therapist, which is intended to keep the level of tension high throughout the treatment and to directly overcome most of the patient's resistances. The patient is directly challenged and confronted with evidence of his or her resistance, so that resistances are often attacked rather than interpreted. This is not to say that the usual techniques of psychotherapy such as interpretations and support are not used when indicated. Indeed, the result of the confrontation is that the genetic material flows more easily and can then be interpreted and understood by the patient. In addition to gaining both an intellectual and an emotional understanding of his or her conflicts, the patient is expected to make real changes in his or her life during the course of treatment. Sifneos does not use a specific time limit, but indicates to the patient that the treatment will be brief. Most patients complete their therapy between 12 and 16 sessions and none go beyond 20 sessions. When the primary conflict is an oedipal one, as it is with most of Sifneos' patients, termination issues are not an important part of the treatment.

Mann

In 1964 James Mann (1973) developed his time-limited psychotherapy in response to the problem of long waiting lists in the psychiatric clinics of the Boston University School of Medicine. His technique is based on his understanding of the normal development of the sense of time. In the young child, time is limitless. One of the tasks of maturation is to realize and accept that time is finite and that life must end. Mann believes that a brief therapy, with a definite time limit, will allow the patient to recapitulate this maturational process in a more adaptive manner than was possible during the patient's childhood.

Mann uses a fixed time limit of 12 sessions. Telling the patient that he can be helped in such a brief period of time reawakens the patient's early feelings of omnipotence, so that the first phase of treatment is characterized by positive feelings about the treatment and rapid symptom amelioration. During the middle phase of treatment, reality, in the form of the impending end of therapy, intrudes and there is disillusionment and ambivalence. In the final phase of treatment the issues of ending the therapy, separating from the therapist, and realizing that time is finite all come together. Whereas the 12-session time limit determines the phases of the treatment, the content is dependent on the focus, which is dependent on the focus that is selected by the patient and the therapist. Mann calls the focus the "central issue." It is determined on the basis of the therapist's understanding of the patient's psychodynamic history and is presented to the patient in terms of some conscious feeling that is connected both to the current presenting symptoms and to the underlying conflict.

Mann's technique has wide application, with only psychotic and borderline individuals definitely excluded. Although Mann recently tried to define his selection process more clearly (Mann and Goldman 1982), he has still not established definite criteria for selection. Psychological-mindedness is not a requirement, so less sophisticated patients can be treated with this technique. The therapy itself is conducted in a nonthreatening manner. The usual psychotherapy techniques of interpretation of defense and impulse are used, though emphasis is on the derivatives of the early conflicts rather than attempting to interpret the core conflict itself. Much attention is paid to the issue of termination as it relates to the central issue and to transference.

Davanloo

Habib Davanloo began his work on brief psychotherapy at the Montreal General Hospital in 1962. Although he has written extensively (Davanloo 1978, 1979, 1980), he has not yet described his technique in a detailed and systematic fashion. Davanloo's technique has a wide application, and he is able to treat individuals who would be rejected by other brief psychotherapists because of the severity of their psychopathology.

The unique feature of Davanloo's technique is his relentless pursuit of even minor resistances of the patient, particularly as they appear in relation to the therapist. Davanloo persists in focusing the patient's attention on the resistance, and especially on the affect, usually anger, that accompanies it. As a result of this persistence, the affect is eventually mobilized and expressed. After this process is repeated many times, the resistance diminishes and material relating to the underlying conflicts that brought the patient to therapy begins to emerge and is dealt with using the usual techniques of psychotherapy. Davanloo works first with the reactions to the therapist, then with reactions to significant others, and finally with the same patterns of reaction in relation to people from the past.

Patients are selected during an evaluation process that is, in effect, a trial therapy. The same technique of mobilizing the patient's hidden affects is used, and if the patient responds with regression rather than with new material, he is not selected. Other factors such as intelligence, ego-strengths, psychological-mindedness, and the quality of the patient's object relations are also considered. Treatments range from 5 to 40 sessions, depending on the severity of the psychopathology and on the experience of the therapist. No definite time limit is set at the start of the treatment.

Current Status of Brief Psychotherapy

The above mentioned brief psychotherapies were all developed independently of one another, and each method has its advocates and its disciples. At this time there is a consensus in the profession (though no hard data) that brief psychotherapy can be an effective modality of therapy for some patients. What is not clear is whether any of the techniques described above are superior to any of the others, whether certain techniques are superior for certain groups of patients, or whether the best features of each technique can be combined in some sort of generally accepted and unified brief psychotherapy technique. Research is currently underway to help answer some of these questions (Trujillo 1985).

References

Alexander, F., and French, T. M. (1946). *Psychoanalytic Psychotherapy*. New York: The Ronald Press.

Breuer, J., and Freud, S. (1895). Studies on hysteria. *Standard Edition* 2:x–305. London: Hogarth Press.

Davanloo, H. (1979). Techniques of short-term dynamic psychotherapy. *Psychiatry Clinics of North America* 2:11–22.

_____ (1980). *Short-Term Dynamic Psychotherapy*. New York: Jason Aronson.

_____, ed. (1978). *Basic Principles and Techniques in Short-Term Dynamic Psychotherapy*. New York: SP Medical and Scientific Books.

Ferenczi, S. (1952). *Further Contributions to the Theory and Technique of Psychoanalysis*, pp. 177–229. New York: Basic Books.

Ferenczi, S., and Rank, O. (1925). *The Development of Psychoanalysis*. New York: Nervous and Mental Disease Publishing Company.

Flegenheimer, W. V. (1982). *Techniques of Brief Psychotherapy*. New York: Jason Aronson.

Freud, S. (1905). A case of hysteria. *Standard Edition* 7:7–122. London: Hogarth Press.

_____ (1937). Analysis terminable and interminable. *Standard Edition* 23:216–253. London: Hogarth Press.

Gill, M. M. (1982). *Analysis of transference*. Vol. I. *Theory and technique*. Psychological issues: Monograph 53.

Jones, E. (1957). *The Life and Work of Sigmund Freud*. 3:56–77. New York: Basic Books.

Malan, D. H. (1963). *A Study of Brief Psychotherapy*. New York: Plenum Press.

_____ (1976a). *The Frontier of Brief Psychotherapy*. New York: Plenum Press.

_____ (1976b). *Towards the Validation of Dynamic Psychotherapy*. New York: Plenum Press.

Mann, J. (1973). *Time-Limited Psychotherapy*. Cambridge: Harvard University Press.

Marmor, J. (1979). Short-term dynamic psychotherapy. *American Journal of Psychiatry*. 136:149–155.

Sifneos, P. E. (1972). *Short-Term Psychotherapy and Emotional Crisis*. Cambridge: Harvard University Press.

_____ (1979). *Short-Term Dynamic Psychotherapy*. New York: Plenum Press.

Sterba, R. (1951). A case of brief psychotherapy by Sigmund Freud. *Psychoanalytic Review* 38:75–80.

Trujillo, M. (1985). Research issues in short-term dynamic psychotherapy. In *Clinical and Research Issues in Short-Term Dynamic Psychotherapy*, ed. A. Winston. Washington, D.C.: American Psychiatric Press.

Chapter 2

THE OEDIPUS COMPLEX

ALTHEA J. HORNER, PH.D.

Short-term therapy does not permit the luxury of an exploratory, "wait and see" attitude. It demands a plan of action based on clear-cut formulations leading to specific goals. Psychoanalytic theory has been built on the data of observation and clinical experience. Short-term treatment reverses this process and entails a vigorous application of theory to the clinical situation. The selection of patients on the basis of the applicability of this theory is critical to the treatment process. The theory is the basis for our psychodynamic formulations, for the definition of our goals, and for our treatment strategies.

The approach to short-term treatment described in this book follows the work of Sifneos (1979), with its concentration on the Oedipus complex as it is manifest in the patient's developmental history, in his or her current life situation, and in the transference. The therapist's concentration and focus on oedipal issues rapidly heats up the treatment situation, generating anxiety and oedipal transference on the part of the patient and, at times, countertransference reactions and anxiety on the part of the therapist. The interventions that bring this about are derived from the therapist's understanding of the nature of the Oedipus complex and its resolution — or "dissolution," according to Freud (1924).

As in long-term therapy, we have with the short-term approach the four phases of (1) uncovering, (2) working through, (3) resolution, and (4) termination. The steps necessary for the resolution of the Oedipus complex have been "operationalized" for purposes of evaluating progress as well as to indicate what must yet be dealt with in treatment. A summary of these steps is shown in Table 1 (pp. 28–29). The steps are based on existing theoretical formulations, as well as on clinical experience.

Uncovering

The work of the uncovering phase of treatment will bring into awareness the wishes and fantasies of the oedipal period: the wish to either have sexually the parent of the opposite sex or to be the preferred object by that parent. Although some patients may never acknowledge the sexual component of the wish, they can acknowledge the competitive wish to be special. They may also be aware of the specialness inherent in the sexual relationship and be angry that they were unable to compete because of the incest taboo. Along with the wish to be preferred by the parent of the opposite sex is the wish to defeat the rival, the parent of the same sex. In cases of extreme ambivalence, this competitive wish may have murderous overtones.

Associated fears that accompany the oedipal strivings need to be understood in terms of their role in the establishment of certain defenses against these strivings, whether they be neurotic and symptomatic, or characterological. These fears may be the loss of control of the intensely experienced impulses, a fear that will be exacerbated by uncertainty as to the reliability of the controls of the opposite-sex parent. Fear of punishment or retaliation by the same-sex parent depends on the quality of that relationship as well as on the fantasy fears of the child. Punishment by either parent may be withdrawal of love, or there may be castration anxiety as well. Fear of punishment of the superego, i.e., guilt also motivates defenses against the oedipal strivings.

Along with impulse and fantasy, the oedipal child (and later the oedipal patient) has to deal with feelings that are associated with the inevitable frustration of infantile wishes. Feelings associated with the opposite-sex parent are anger, feelings of betrayal, a sense of failure or inadequacy, as well as sadness and yearning. Feelings evoked by the rival are those of envy and/or humiliation.

Working Through

With the uncovering of the several facets of the conflict itself, the patient develops insight into the manner in which these conflicts are played out both in everyday life and in the transference. They can be seen to interfere with the establishment of satisfying heterosexual relationships and with the achievement of goals and ambitions, as competitiveness must be inhibited and defended against.

With these insights there has to be a renunciation of the infantile strivings along with an acceptance of the parents as real people. This means letting go of the idealization and/or disparagement of either or both parents which were part of the fantasies and the defenses against them.

Recall Freud's (1923) observation that as the object-cathexes of parental objects are relinquished, they are replaced by identifications, both as part of the ego and as the nucleus of the superego. The acknowledgment and acceptance of these identifications are essential to the resolution of the Oedipus complex. Identification with the opposite-sex parent no longer will jeopardize gender identity, and identification with either parent will be freed from contamination by negative perception of the parent, rendering those identifications no longer a danger to the ego-ideal.

The concept of penis envy is anathema to feminists of all ages and is ego-alien to women with a strong feminine identification who are in conflict over identifying with the father and resist doing so. Instead, they cling to the wish to have him as the libidinal object. Yet, moving past that point in analysis of the eroticization of father's power, to the recognition that the woman holds her husband responsible for providing her the power and prestige she previously felt vicariously through her attachment to her father, we must address the issue of the envy of that power and prestige and the competitive wish to have one's own. Clinically we may see that the competitive issues are evident between the girl and her father and between the woman and her husband and her boss. Clinging to the wish to be

Table 1. Steps Necessary to Resolve the Oedipus Complex

STEPS	OPPOSITE-SEX PARENT	SAME-SEX PARENT
1. Uncovering		
Acknowledge wish, fantasy, or desire	To have sexually and/or to be the preferred object	To defeat in competition and to displace; to murder
Understand fear associated with the wish	Loss of control	Punishment (e.g., castration or withdrawal of love); guilt
Understand negative affect associated with frustration	Anger; feelings of betrayal; sense of failure or inadequacy; sadness, yearning	Humiliation; envy
2. Working Through		
Insight into how conflicts are played out (a) in present day life (b) in the transference	Interference with heterosexual relationships	Interference with achievement of goals and ambitions

3. Resolution

Renunciation of the wish	To have sexually and/or to be the preferred object	To defeat in competition and to displace
Acceptance of parents as real people	Without the need to idealize or disparage	Without the need to idealize or disparage
Acknowledgment of identifications	With opposite-sex parent without endangerment of gender identity and/or the ego ideal	With same-sex parent without endangerment of the ego-ideal
Neutralization of drive	Desexualization of affection toward parent of opposite sex	De-aggressivization of strivings for success and achievement
Redirection of strivings	To new love object. Reunion of sex and affection without guilt or anxiety	Toward ambitions. Strivings for success and achievement without guilt or anxiety

4. Termination

Therapist is perceived in realistic terms as adult equal	Patient withdraws emotional investment in treatment and redirects it toward his real life	Patient actively takes over full responsibility for own life

special by being nice and helpful, she passively and defensively continues to derive that power vicariously, envying it, enraged when it is not forthcoming, but still disclaiming the wish for her own. Returning to the issue within the family where her father was both adored and seen as weak in the power balance with a domineering mother, one patient was able to see that she still idealized her father's maleness. The concept of maleness is less likely to be rejected as a source of envy than the concrete symbol of the penis.

P: I want the status, but I don't want to work to earn it. But I don't want it given to me when I don't earn it.

T: The man just *is* powerful. You have to *do something* to be powerful. But then you would be more like a man.

P: Right. Should we talk about my father?

T: Does something come to mind?

P: I always get the same picture of that incident when I was on my knees at his feet reading and he uncrossed his legs and accidentally kicked me. He didn't know I was there. I made a big fuss and cried. He was surprised. I cried, but I think I enjoyed having that lump on my lip, like my medical emergency. That was really being special. There was pleasure in it. It was the most exciting thing that ever happened to me.

T: Like the lump on your lip. What did that mean interpersonally, with you and your father?

P: I wanted to show he did something bad, maybe to prove he was a bad person. Maybe to break away from the feeling that he was wonderful.

T: Why did you need to do that?

P: I didn't want to think it. It was babyish. Or I was ashamed of how I felt about him. It was a weapon he had. If I cared about his feeling for me, he could control me. I looked for a reason not to care.

T: You envied what you admired and needed to bring it down.

P: I could see it in relation to his being male, the envy. I tried to show him as being less. That makes a lot of

sense that a little girl in *my* house would want to be
male. Though I'm glad to be a woman. It's easier. The
trying and exerting part of being male is what I don't
want. I don't want to be a man, but wish to have that —
the aggressiveness. I think I'm developing it more. But
the conflict is deep and severe and mysterious.

Eventually, the woman must be able to own her identifications
with the admired father without feeling her gender identity compro-
mised if she is to be able to give up the father equivalent as the object of her infantile libidinal strivings. It is not the penis she wants
but the power and status attributed to her father's maleness, which
she must assimilate into her femaleness by identifying with it in an
ego-syntonic way.

Resolution

Resolution of the Oedipus complex entails neutralization of drive,
the de-sexualization of affection toward the parent of the opposite
sex and the de-aggressivization of strivings for success and achievement. Concomitantly, there will be a redirection of those strivings
away from the early objects toward a new love object, with the re-
union of sex and affection without guilt or anxiety, as well as toward
the ambitions without guilt or anxiety.

Termination

With termination and resolution of the transference, the therapist
will be experienced in realistic terms, as an adult equal. There should
be a concomitant withdrawal of the emotional investment in treatment with a redirection of emotional energy toward real life. At the
same time, the patient now actively takes full responsibility for his/
her life. This step forward may generate its own guilt insofar as it
constitutes what Loewald (1979) calls a kind of parricide, an overthrow of the authority of the parents.

Although these steps are presented in a specific order, in practice our patients do not always obey our formulations so closely. Nevertheless, if the overall schema is well understood by the therapist, he or she will be able to move freely with the patient with respect to which of the issues is in the forefront and still maintain the focus on the oedipal issues throughout treatment. In the following chapters, the clinical application of this schema is described in detail.

Presented in this chapter is an expanded theoretical formulation of the oedipal situation as it dovetails with the final stage of the separation-individuation process (Mahler, Pine, and Bergman 1975). A clear understanding of the latter is essential if the therapist is not to be lured back into preoedipal issues, a strategic error of the first magnitude in oedipally focused, short-term treatment.

Identification and Structuralization of the Ego and Superego

Identification is the process common to the completion of the separation-individuation process and to the resolution of the Oedipus complex. Freud (1923) wrote that with the dissolution of the Oedipus complex, there will be both a mother-identification and a father-identification. The identification with the father both replaces the object-relation with him and preserves the object-relation with the mother, whereas the identification with the mother replaces the object-relation with her and preserves that with the father.

But Freud (1921) notes that there is an earlier identification with the parent of the same sex that sets the stage for the Oedipus complex. The little boy wants to be like his father, who he takes as his ideal. This is typical of little boys. The object cathexis of the early mother and this identification with the masculine father exist side by side for a time with no mutual influence or interference. The normal Oedipus complex, Freud notes, originates from their confluence. When the little boy becomes aware that his father stands between him and his mother, the identification takes on a hostile coloring and becomes identical with the wish to replace the father. Just as identification may be an expression of tenderness, so can it readily turn into a competitive wish for the removal of the other. That is, the identification may stand as a substitute for the actual love relationship, or it may make the relationship unnecessary, rendering the other a rival.

Freud (1923) anticipated modern object relational thinking when he wrote that the character of the ego is a precipitate of abandoned object cathexes and that it contains the history of those past choices. He noted, "It may be that this identification is the sole condition under which the id can give up its object" (p. 29).

Identification as a process leading to a change in the structure of the ego must be distinguished from the kind of gross identification that serves as an ego defense against object loss or other dangers to the ego. The internalizations that allow one to *give up* the object are not the same as the identifications that *defend against* the anxiety and depression of loss. An example of the latter would be the identification with a depressed or suffering mother. I have seen patients who reacted to the death of a mother during their late childhood or adolescent years by taking on, in toto, the personality of the mother as they viewed it. Defensive identification does not lead to a structural change in the self-representation. Developmental identifications do.

In his discussion of the relationship between identification and individuation, Schecter (1968) defines the process of identification as *"the means by which part of the psychic structure of one person tends to become like that of another to whom he is emotionally related in a significant way"* (p. 50). He elaborates further saying that identification can also be conceived as a *"relatively enduring modification of the self in the direction of similarity to the object as it is perceived and 'personified' by the ego."*

Schecter also distinguishes the conscious wish to become like another person, as happens in the formation of one's ideals, from the actual tendency to become like another; that is, from the basic developmental processes leading to structural likeness. He also distinguishes both of these from "pseudoidentification," which involves an attempt to reconstruct an internalized object with which the self may then fuse. "The severely disturbed, often psychotic patient attempts to cling to the internal object, to fuse with it, to 'become' it, or to destroy it" (p. 74). In the evaluation of the patient in either long- or short-term treatment, we must be able to differentiate normal, developmental identification from defensive or "pseudoidentification."

Schecter concludes that identification grows out of primarily active and relatively conflict-free individuating processes and that it contributes to the ego structure or strength that is necessary for the gradual relinquishing of the more primitive object ties: that is, "Identification and the partial loosening of primitive object attachments may be simultaneous and part and parcel of the same individuation process. . . . " (p. 64).

Freud saw the identifications that mark the dissolution of the Oedipus complex as forming a precipitate in the ego which consists of the two identifications (with mother and father) as in some way united with each other. This modification of the ego, he says, then "confronts the other contents of the ego as an ego-ideal or superego."

Identification and Object Constancy

The end of the separation-individuation process (Mahler, Pine, and Bergman 1975) is marked by a fully established sense of a separate identity and object constancy. Object constancy is the outcome of a series of internalizations of parental, and particularly maternal, functions and modalities (Tolpin 1971, Giovacchini 1979). From an object-relational viewpoint, failures of identification result in an ego insufficiency that constitutes the port of entry to preoedipal symptomatology in a regressive fashion. This insufficiency—the incomplete securing of object constancy—is the basis for an ongoing dependency vis-a-vis the object, for the lack of full intrapsychic autonomy that generates fears of abandonment, separation-anxiety, and depression (Horner 1979, 1984).

Burgner and Edgcumbe (1972) understand the concept of object constancy as "the individual's capacity to differentiate between objects and to maintain a relationship to one specific object regardless of whether needs are being satisfied or not . . . " (p. 315). It is the "capacity to recognize and tolerate loving and hostile feelings toward the same object; the capacity to keep feelings centered on a specific object; and the capacity to value an object for attributes other than its functions of satisfying needs" (p. 328).

Eventually this must entail the ability to see parents as they really are without a dependent idealization or a defensive disparagement.

This constitutes one of the steps in the resolution of the Oedipus complex.

Mahler describes object constancy in terms of the internal good object, the maternal image that is psychically available to the child just as the actual mother was previously available for sustenance, comfort, and love. Mahler et al. comment that object constancy seems to come about during the third year and that with this achievement the mother can be substituted for, in part, by the now reliable internal image. The security that comes with this step toward intrapsychic autonomy makes it possible for the child to sustain the anxieties of the oedipal conflict and thus to maintain the forward thrust of development.

And so the end of the separation-individuation process is marked by the assimilation of maternal functions into the self even as the object is separated out as fully differentiated from the self. This involves not only the assimilation of nurturant and executive modalities, but also of maternal anxiety-reducing interactions that lead to the development of signal anxiety (Horner 1980). The assimilation of the imperatives that leads to the structuring of the superego (Schecter 1979) is an integral aspect of the resolution of the Oedipus complex.

The assimilation of the functions and qualities of the object into the self-representation at this point of development — that is, the process of identification — is thus a sine qua non for the achievement of intrapsychic autonomy and for increasing autonomy vis-a-vis the object relationships of the oedipal period.

With the failure to make the identifications that mark the close of the separation-individuation process, we can anticipate that there will be prominent oedipal issues, since the same identificatory process is essential to its resolution, and since the lack of emotional autonomy will aggravate the anxieties associated with oedipal strivings. Anything that interferes with the identification process will prevent the ultimate resolution of both separation-individuation and the Oedipus complex.

As long as the significant attributes of the object belong to the object rather than to the self, the self will remain dependent on the external object for the provision of these attributes and what they contribute to the security and self-esteem of the individual. Clinically, these patients present with a picture of exaggerated dependency and depression in the context of a relatively well-differentiated and structured ego. These dependencies are often played out in current adult-life relationships, and there is often a clear oedipal cast to them as well.

The Refusal to Identify: Guardian of the Ego-Ideal and Gender Identity

I have observed that in the male, the need to protect the sense of masculinity is a deterrent to the identifications with mother that are essential to intrapsychic autonomy. Greenson (1968) writes of the importance of disidentifying from mother for the little boy in the service of securing his male gender identity. Greenson uses the term "disidentify" in his discussion of the little boy's struggle to free himself from the early symbiotic fusion with mother. "The male child's ability to disidentify will determine the success or failure of his later identification with father. These two phenomena, disidentifying with mother and counteridentifying with father, are interdependent and form a complementary series" (p. 306). The outcome of this process is determined by the mother's willingness to let the boy identify with the father figure and by the motives the father offers the child for identifying with him. Part of the motivation to identify with father also arises out of the mother's love and respect for the father. This process is often made near impossible when the real qualities of the father — e.g., an alcoholic father — make him unacceptable as a model for the boy. Oedipal anxieties also interfere with the boy's identification with the father inasmuch as competitive strivings may thereby be intensified and made more dangerous *to the father*, whom the boy also loves and wishes to preserve.

Greenson poses the question: What happens to the original identification with the mother? He wonders if it disappears or becomes latent. And, he asks, "How much of the boy's identification with the father is a counteridentification, actually a 'contra'-identification, a means of counteracting the earlier identification?" (p. 312). Greenson postulates that it is in this area that we may find an answer as to why so many men are uncertain about their maleness. I pose an additional question: "What is the relationship between the inability of many men to experience and express tender emotions and an early splitting off and repression of identifications with the nurturant mother in the service of protecting their sense of maleness?"

I believe that it is this very need to disidentify with the mother to protect the sense of maleness that precludes the achievement of object constancy and intrapsychic autonomy. Because he is then thrust into an often covert dependent relationship with his object relationships in adult life, oedipal anxieties are inherent in the relationships as well.

A 35-year-old unmarried man complained of not being able to establish a lasting relationship with a woman. On the basis of his positive identifications with his loved and admired father, he was able to achieve a high level of business success. However, he still maintained a posture of inadequacy with respect to certain executive functions and strengths attributed to the mother, a posture he played out in his relationships with women, inviting their domination and contempt. The issue of his fear of identifying with mother and the dangers associated with his oedipal fantasies had been under exploration before the session from which the following excerpt is taken.

> P: It's the issue of being inferior or superior. I discussed it in my relationship to you. I never felt superior — at times inferior and at times a peer — but never superior. Being superior gives me an overblown sense of myself and of controlling the other by being patronizing or protective. Or there's a sense of inadequacy when I feel less, when I feel incompetent, unable to do something. When I feel inadequate and less than myself, I acquire characteristics of the other, and there's a role confusion. It's hard to separate myself from you. When I feel inadequate, I need to acquire the strength of the other.

> T: By becoming that person.

> P: And not a separate entity. I need to identify the elements of my dependency and work on them. In enough of my relationship with you I feel inadequate. I wish your strength to be mine. I rely on your judgment.

> T: The trick will be to learn from my strength and make it part of you and still be able to maintain your sense of separateness from me.

P: I still need to identify what you got that I ain't got, and why I feel I don't have it. If I can come to terms with it I will have the ability to relinquish my need to acquire your strength, yielding the separateness.

T: Because you had to hold on to your sense of maleness as a boy, you couldn't let yourself acquire your mother's strength.

P: The achievement of maleness is also the problem of losing the the strength she represents to me in terms of emotional self-sufficiency. Like my apartment—if I wasn't fearful of identifying with her I would have been able to acquire her strength in this area. I saw NOT taking care of my apartment as a rebellion and as positive. I was determined to be male and to be independent.

Oedipal issues were predominant with this man. Fantasies of intercourse with mother led to fantasies not only of castration—by mother—but also of annihilation of a separate self. Fantasies of killing father so he could have mother evoked anxiety because he perceived his father, and his identification with him, as rescuing him from the engulfing preoedipal mother. He remained dependent because he could not allow identifications with mother that would lead to intrapsychic autonomy. With the dependency he perceived her (women) as strong, and he wanted her (their) strength. He could only imagine his gaining it through an identificatory merger (pseudoidentification), or by destroying the woman and stealing her power from her, which led to feelings of guilt and anxiety.

Loewald (1979) pays attention to the interaction of oedipal and preoedipal issues and notes that the incest barrier is a barrier between identification and object cathexis. Particularly in the boy, "the preoedipal stage of primary lack of subject/object differentiation is evolving into the object stage. . . . The incestuous object, thus, is an intermediate, ambiguous entity, neither a full-fledged libidinal *objectum* nor an unequivocal *identificatum*" (pp. 766–767). In the treatment of the patient described above, the fears of annihilation beyond castration that went with the fantasies of intercourse with mother illustrate the more terrifying oedipal dangers for the boy.

Oedipal strivings pull the little girl away from the mother of primary identification and, if anything, emphasize the separation.

In this instance, rejection of the identifications with mother leads to a failure to achieve object constancy.

The relative infrequency of mother-son incest and the sense that it indicates far greater pathology than father-daughter incest are very likely related to the preoedipal merger issues inherent in the act. This fear is also reflected in the social norms that allow older man–younger woman alliances, but frown upon those between older women and younger men. Ridicule of the situation reveals the emotional discomfort, particularly for men, of the evoked fantasies of mother-son incest. Freud (1917a, p. 335) noted that mother incest and parricide were the two great crimes proscribed by totemism, the first socio-religious institution of mankind.

We need to distinguish the primary identifications that originate in the symbiotic bond of early object relations development and the later identifications that come with the resolution of the Oedipus complex. Loewald notes, "If . . . parents foster the predominance of incestuous trends, that development is interfered with. The older, primary identifications inherent in the incestuous trends are then not allowed to become partially transformed into superego identifications, as the oedipal relationship is not relinquished but perpetuated" (p. 767). When the oedipal-incestuous ties are relinquished and when the restitutive identification with aspects of the oedipal objects leads to superego formation, "it is implied that to a significant degree primary identifications give way to secondary or superego identifications."

Freud thought that the identifications at the end of the oedipal period were not so much with the actual egos of the parents as with *their* superegos. The picture of the parents that is incorporated is often distorted by virtue of the child's fantasies and colored by his or her own projected sadistic impulses.

Loewald comments that in the classical neuroses, what he calls the "psychotic core" (that is, the residuals of the primary identifications in the unconscious) may not need specific analytic work. This is a basic assumption in the selection of patients for short-term treatment focused on the Oedipus complex.

Freud (1931) commented that he had given up any expectation of a neat parallelism between male and female sexual development. The little boy's tender attachment to his mother alongside a hostile attitude to his father is easy to understand inasmuch as his mother was his first love object. But, Freud adds, "With the little girl it is different. Her first love object, too, was her mother." And he attempts to understand how the little girl then finds her way to the father. "How, when and why does she detach herself from her mother?" (p. 225).

He answers this by saying that "the female only reaches the normal positive Oedipus situation after she has surmounted a period that is governed by the negative complex. And indeed during that phase a little girl's father is not much else for her than a troublesome rival" (p. 226). Freud views the development to womanhood as based in the carrying over of the little girl's affective object attachments from her mother to her father. The long-range implications he notes, saying:

> . . . we noticed that many women who have chosen their husband on the model of their father, or have put him in their father's place, nevertheless repeat towards him, in their married life, their bad relations with their mother. The husband of such a woman was meant to be the inheritor of her relation to her father, but in reality he became the inheritor of her relation to her mother. (p. 230).

Freud says of the little girl's love for her mother that it comes to grief because of the many disappointments that are unavoidable and that lead to an accumulation of aggression toward the mother. These "griefs," according to Freud, are (1) the frustration of the wish for exclusivity vis-a-vis the mother and the jealousy of siblings as well as of father, who are her rivals; (2) the frustration of sexuality that is experienced when mother prohibits masturbation, even though mother, in her cleaning and toileting of the child, arouses her sexual feelings; (3) the depreciation of the idealized mother when the little girl depreciates femaleness in general because of the inherent implications of castration; (4) the anger at the mother for not giving her a penis; and, finally, (5) anger that mother did not give her enough milk or suckle her long enough. Freud did not see the hostile attitude of girls toward their mothers as a consequence of the oedipal rivalry, but as originating in the preceding phase and then transformed and exploited in the oedipal situation. The idealization of the oedipal father also evokes a corresponding depreciation of mother who loses out in the comparison, or mother is wishfully devalued as a rival for father, with fantasies of a "good self" as necessarily triumphant.

The mother must also be de-idealized as part of the little girl's strivings toward autonomy and individuation from the primary attachment object. This was manifest transferentially in the treatment of a woman who noted she had had to make her mother bad in order to separate from her. The same issue arose in the termination phase of her analysis.

With the little girl's multiply-determined need to disparage the mother, there is an aborting of the identifications essential to the achievement of object constancy and intrapsychic autonomy, and the girl-woman maintains the dependent stance vis-a-vis the new object, i.e., the idealized oedipal father and later male love objects.

The refusal to identify with the now disparaged mother stands as a guardian of the ego-ideal. That is, identification with her would lead to a disparaged sense of self as well. The refusal to identify also functions as a defense against the dangers of the oedipal situation, inasmuch as the daughter perceives certain qualities or abilities as belonging to the mother and forbidden to her, as taboo as her wishes for her father. Not only is mother the only one who is allowed to be sexual, she is the only one who is allowed to be talented, to be strong, or to be whatever else has been designated as mother's domain. Competitive strivings of any sort are guilt-ridden and repressed because of their close association with oedipal strivings. We find the predominant defense mechanism in instances of refusal to identify to be reaction formation. Not only am I not like mother, I am just the opposite.

It became clear in the course of a long-term psychoanalytic psychotherapy with a middle-aged homosexual woman that her relationships with women were based on her fear of them and her attempt to placate them. Her associations, memories, and dreams strongly suggested a heterosexual character.

The departure of the father from the home when she was 5 years old threw her back upon her dependent tie with a narcissistic and exploitative mother. Her relationships with women had been predominantly masochistic, with a hope that by pleasing and placating, she would be loved and not abandoned. As Freud noted, when the father is disappointing, the little girl will return to the attachment to the mother and to the sexuality of the negative Oedipus complex.

In treatment she experienced severe anxiety whenever she reported a pleasant or gratifying experience. Transferentially the therapist was experienced as the envious mother who would not tolerate her having anything good. She tended to offer gifts in a seductive manner in those situations when her anger threatened to emerge from repression.

As termination began to be discussed, she reported two dreams.

> One dream was violent. Someone had been killed and I
> needed a note to say that I wasn't present. In the second
> dream I was in a therapy session. The therapist didn't look
> like you, but it was you. There were a lot of people around.
> I got angry. I said I wouldn't pay when I had to share and
> be interrupted.

Her anger at her mother who failed to meet her needs, who went out with boyfriends, and who left her with the responsibility of younger siblings is evident in these dreams. She experienced the idea of termination as an abandonment, even though she had initiated the topic. The patients who would be staying with the therapist in treatment were the envied siblings. The guilt and the need to deny the anger was expressed in the first dream.

Toward the end of her treatment she became romantically involved with a man. He responded to her in a manner that allowed her to re-experience the lost bond of tender affection and sexuality she once had with her father. At this time she began to experience the coming termination as punishment for her relationship with a man. She reported being strongly drawn to a woman and offered dreams that said, in effect, "I still only want women — that is, I still only want you, Mother." Interpretation mitigated the anxiety and the flight from her emerging heterosexual interests.

It also became clear that her renunciation of strength with all its feared ramifications left her dependent upon the powerful maternal figure. The renunciation was partly due to her fear of her aggression as well as a view of her mother's aggression as bad. In all events, she would be "nicer" than her mother was. Her need to hold on to an image of herself that she came to characterize as "goody two-shoes," prevented the internalization of mother's strength in its positive and effective significance. The need to protect this image of an unrealistic "sanctified" self was addressed throughout the course of her treatment.

That the inhibition of aggression was also tied to oedipal issues is clear from the following dream.

> There was a woman, my mother. She was pregnant and married to her second husband. In the scene I seduced him. I kissed him and held his body close to mine. I enjoyed it. I didn't care that my mother was there.

After relating the dream she asserted rather fiercely that she had no intentions of letting mother keep her from what she wanted in life any more. It should be noted that her mother was no longer living at this time. With the acceptance of the real mother and a more realistic view of her nature, the patient was able to internalize the strength that had only been allowed to mother and that had also been viewed as bad. With this shift she began to think in terms of ending treatment with far less ambivalence and with a sense of accomplishment. With the resolution of the competitive need to devalue mother, the patient could acknowledge the identifications necessary to emotional autonomy.

The "Complete" Oedipus Complex

Freud (1923) distinguished what he calls the simple, positive Oedipus complex in a boy—an ambivalent attitude to the father and object-relation of a solely affectionate kind to his mother—from the complete Oedipus complex in which there is also an ambivalent attitude to the mother and an affectionate object-choice toward the father. The same dual strivings would be true of the little girl. Freud writes:

> In my opinion it is advisable in general . . . to assume the existence of the complete Oedipus complex. . . . At the dissolution of the Oedipus complex the four trends of which it consists will group themselves in such a way as to produce a father-identification and a mother-identification. (p. 33)

There is implicit in the concept of the complete Oedipus complex a bisexual potentiality in every child. The ultimate course of development will depend not only on the balance of parental forces during the oedipal period, but also on the vicissitudes of earlier object relations development.

It has been my experience in the treatment of homosexual women that there are two groups. One group, like the woman described above, are bisexual in behavior as well as in the dream life, and it becomes clear that they have retreated from the dangers of the oedipal situation. For these women the dangers were those of maternal abandonment alongside an unavailable father. Furthermore, potential maternal narcissistic rage led these daughters to a stance of placating the feared and needed female, behavior evident in their adult homosexual relationships. They more fear women than love them.

In the heterosexual development of the female child, the oedipal father, if emotionally available, may become a substitute for an unavailable mother (or for the mother actively rejected by the little girl), and there will be a fusion of dependency and oedipal strivings vis-a-vis the male. Because of the disruption of the line of development through the primary attachment to the mother, the achievement of object constancy is aborted.

The second group of homosexual women whom I have treated are those with a character disorder — either a narcissistic personality or a borderline character. Oedipal strivings, if we can call them that, have as their aim the undifferentiated mother. That is, sexual strivings were assimilated into the incompletely differentiated self and object constellation. The symbiotic-like quality of their adult relationships is also marked in the transference. The need/demand for merger, for total mirroring, and the rage when it was not forthcoming are in strong contrast to the more highly differentiated stance in the transference of the first group. In their interpersonal relationships, triangular situations have the same competitive cast as in the positive Oedipus complex situation, although perhaps possessiveness is a better word than competitive. We need to distinguish what here is essentially a dyadic setup and not a triangular one insofar as the third person has no significant relational meaning to the individual. The concept of an earlier negative Oedipus complex in the female as described by Freud is thus open to question in these instances. Can we apply a triadic concept to a dyadic situation?

All in all, since positive oedipal strivings pull the little girl away from the preoedipal mother, we can regard them as essentially progressive. On the other hand, the oedipal wishes of the little boy pull him back toward the preoedipal mother and stand in opposition to his drive toward individuation; that is, they tend to have a regressive impact. I would hypothesize that the little boy who turns to his father as oedipal object-choice must do so, in some cases, to counter the threat to the loss of separateness vis-a-vis the primary attachment object, the mother. It is a flight from engulfment and annihilation of the separate self. At the same time, a secondary identification with the mother compensates for her loss. The inverted complex in the male child may also come about in the context of an emotionally unavailable mother vis-a-vis a more available father. Blos (1984) conceptualizes the negative complex in boys as dyadic, i.e., the boy's preambivalent attachment to the father whose love enables him to escape the engulfment of the preoedipal mother.

In effect, then, the father as oedipal object-choice assists individuation and/or substitutes for the inadequate mother for both boys and girls. The specific balance of maternal and paternal emotional availability as well as their support of individuation will be unique to each situation, and the outcome of any line of development can be understood in those terms if we look at the situation with minute care.

The Fate of the Oedipus Complex

Freud (1913, 1917a) noted that analysis of adult neurotics reveals the unresolved Oedipus complex and came to the conclusion that it was the nucleus of the neuroses.

With puberty, when the sexual demands are experienced in their full strength, the old familiar incestuous objects are once again cathected with libido. The adolescent is faced with the task of detaching himself from his parents, and Freud asserts that it is not until that task is achieved that the individual can cease to be a child and take his or her place in the social community. This task involves giving up the libidinal attachment to the parent of the opposite sex and reconciling himself or herself with the parent of the same sex. He says of the neurotic solution:

> . . . no solution at all is arrived at: the son remains all his life
> bowed beneath his father's authority and he is unable to transfer
> his libido to an outside sexual object (p. 336).

Freud (1924, p. 177) notes that what he calls the "dissolution" of the Oedipus complex is more than a repression, and that if indeed, the "ego has in fact not achieved more than a *repression* of the complex, the latter persists in an unconscious state in the id and will later manifest its pathogenic effect." These are the pathogenic effects, as they interfere with the capacity both to love and to sustain an intimate adult sexual relationship and with the capacity to achieve one's goals and ambitions (i.e., the conflictual nature of competition and success), that we observe in the patients who are identified as candidates for short-term, oedipally focused psychotherapy.

Freud notes that the absence of success of the oedipal strivings leads both the boy and the girl to turn away from its hopeless longing. He writes that the destruction of the Oedipus complex is primarily brought about by the threat of castration. For the boy there are two ways to satisfaction: the active way in which he puts himself in his father's place and has intercourse with mother as father did, in which case father is a hindrance, and the passive way in which he takes the place of mother and is loved by father, and mother is superfluous. According to Freud, both routes entail castration—the masculine one as punishment and the feminine one as a precondition.

He writes:

> If the satisfaction of love in the field of the Oedipus complex is
> to cost the child his penis, a conflict is bound to arise between his
> narcissistic interest in that part of his body and the libidinal ca-
> thexis of his parental objects. In this conflict the first of these
> forces normally triumphs: the child's ego turns away from the
> Oedipus complex (p. 176).

As the object-cathexes of parental objects are relinquished, they are replaced by identifications. Their authority is taken into the ego and forms the nucleus of the superego, perpetuating the prohibition against incest. The libidinal trends are, in part, de-sexualized and transformed into impulses of affection toward the parents.

Loewald (1979) does not believe that there ever is a final resolution of the Oedipus complex, but comments that there is a "waning" that can be expected both developmentally and as the outcome of treatment. With respect to the outcome of analysis and the establishment of a relationship of equality with one's parents, he says, "it is not established once and for all, but requires continued internal activity; and it is not necessarily obvious at the point of actual termination" (p. 764).

The Superego and the Ego-Ideal

Freud's concept of the ego-ideal changed over time. In his introductory lectures (1917b) he wrote that the ego-ideal is created "for the purpose of recovering thereby the self-satisfaction bound up with the primary infantile narcissism, which since those days has suffered so many shocks and mortification." In object-relational terms, I view this kind of ego-ideal as related to the grandiose self, a defensive and compensatory structure that may be activated by those very "shocks and mortification." A defensive and compensatory ego-ideal must be distinguished from that of the mature superego, which is the outcome of the transmuting internalizations of parental imperatives (Schecter 1979) at the end of the separation-individuation process and with the resolution of the Oedipus complex.

Freud made that shift in 1933 in the "New Introductory Lectures" when the superego was referred to as the "vehicle of the ego ideal." He saw the ego-ideal as derived from the child's perception of the admired parent, "an expression of the admiration which the child felt for the perfection which it at that time ascribed to them."

Sandler, Holder, and Meers (1963) relate the ego-ideal to the ideal self, which they view, in object relational terms, as one of the shapes that the self-representation can assume. They trace the development of a mature, reality-oriented ideal self as it takes place in the healthy individual. They see the ideal self as far more fluid and flexible than are the ideals that were held up to the child by his introjects, even though the ideal self still contains a solid core of identifications with the admired parents of his earliest years. They note that in the healthy individual, the ideal self undergoes continuous modification according to the person's experiences of reality. In states of regression, however, the ideal self becomes more like certain aspects of the idealized pregenital objects. The authors add that parental ideals are modified and displaced over time and integrated with ideals taken over from other figures throughout life. This will apply to what is taken in of the therapist in psychoanalysis. Bromberg (1983) notes that it is not the analyst's functions with which the patient identifies, but the analyst's superego, as perceived by the patient.

The question must be raised about those instances in which the parents were not admired. One woman found substitute models in the idealized television family of "Father Knows Best." There may be a need to reject available identifications to maintain a more primitive ideal with its core of narcissistic perfection. The short-term approach would not be suitable for such a patient, and, indeed, assessment of superego functions is an intrinsic aspect of evaluation for short-term treatment, which requires a core of reliable, realistic self-esteem (see Chapter 5).

Loewald notes that the essence of the superego as an internal agency involves owning up to one's needs and impulses as one's own. This is a necessary step in the uncovering process of therapy. It means "granting them actively that existence which they have in any event with or without our permission" (p. 761). He comments that this involves facing and bearing guilt for acts we consider criminal, even if these acts exist only in fantasy. The criminal acts he refers to are the incestuous fantasies of the Oedipus complex and what he views as a form of parricide: the murder of parental authority and the assumption of responsibility for one's own life that takes place with the severing of the emotional ties with parents. Incest is the "crime" associated with oedipal wishes, and parricide is the "crime" associated with the resolution of the Oedipus complex. "Not only parental authority is destroyed by wresting authority from the parents and taking it over, but the parents, if the process were thoroughly carried out, are being destroyed as libidinal objects as well . . . " (p. 757). He does note that if things go well, what will be left is tenderness, mutual trust, and respect—the signs of equality. Freud too notes that the libidinal trends of the Oedipus complex are de-sexualized, aim-inhibited, and changed into impulses of affection.

Loewald sees the repression of the Oedipus complex as evading the emancipatory murder of the parents and as a way to preserve infantile, libidinal-dependent ties with them. He notes that when parricide is carried out, "aspects of oedipal relations are transformed into superego relations (internalization), and other aspects are, qua relations with external objects, restructured in such a way that the incestuous character of object relations gives way to novel forms of object choice" (p. 758). Even so, he tells us, these novel choices will still be under the influence of those internalizations.

Loewald concludes that oedipal issues are new versions of the basic union-individuation dilemma. "The superego, as the culmination of individual psychic structure formation, represents something ultimate in the basic separation-individuation process" (p. 755).

The Therapeutic Focus: Oedipal or Preoedipal?

Diagnostic considerations for short-term therapy as described in this book demand a high level of development, with no significant character pathology. If we keep in mind that any new developmental phase or event takes place within the context of a preexisting character structure, we can expect that the form and expression of oedipal issues will vary from child to child and from patient to patient. At the emergence of oedipal strivings, one child may still be struggling with the task of differentiation from an engulfing mother. Will the little boy have to withdraw into schizoid detachment to protect his sense of self? Will the little girl so fear object loss that she brings her sexuality to the mother figure? Another child may be consumed with rage at an abandoning mother. Will the boy's frustrated oedipal yearnings fan the flame of his narcissistic rage? Will the little girl sense the anger with which she turns to father, later experiencing her interest in men as a bad and hostile wish? Will she flaunt her involvement with father as a way to torment the mother at whom she is so angry? A more evolved child may have negotiated the tasks of the separation-individuation process, attaining a modicum of object constancy, and as an adult patient, present with some of the more classical issues pertaining to the Oedipus complex.

The oedipal dynamic can be discerned in somewhat altered form in the patient from another culture. An Oriental man, raised in a traditional home, presented with the problem of being unable to advance in his managerial position. His unwillingness to challenge authority, his passive placating behavior, his wish to hide behind a more powerful other were all addressed in the transference and in the work situation. At the 12th session he said he felt something was still missing. Up to that point he had claimed he did not remember his early years. Turning the focus backward in time, he was able to perceive the same dynamics in the family situation.

There was a large extended family living in one household, with the father's older brother the veritable ruler of the clan. The children of this man carried his status as well and challenging them was as forbidden as challenging the uncle. The mother and father bowed to the uncle's authority, although the mother complained bitterly about him.

The patient denied affectional feelings for his mother at first, although later he could say he wanted her love. He was able to experience hatred for the uncle and disappointment in the father who would not stand up to his brother. The worst thing one could do to another was to make that person look bad. The patient recalled the time he did stand up to the uncle on his mother's behalf, wishing to protect her. He acknowledged that there probably was a wish to be special to her. But mother was furious at him for making her look bad, that he, her son, should be so disrespectful to the uncle. The patient was able to say that he felt betrayed by his mother and angry at his father for not backing him up. As he talked about this, he experienced "fear" and then a sense of emptiness.

Although sexuality seemed far from the scene, the wish to be special to mother vis-a-vis a powerful male figure is clear. The failure of the father (by virtue of the cultural demand as well as his own character) to provide a model worthy of emulation led to a wish for the powerful protecting authority figure, as well as the acceptance of the passivity and the development of passive-aggressive strategies. The wish to be special to father was played out in rivalry with his younger brother and centered on money. The father-son dynamic was also being played out with his own son, with the patient angry that his son didn't do well in school, making him look bad. He was also aware that with the model he was providing, he was repeating the very dynamic he hated.

The verbatim record of some of his sessions is reported in Chapter 11.

Assuming that oedipal and preoedipal factors affect one another in a reciprocal fashion and that character structure in terms of object-relations development is a central issue, a developmental diagnosis is essential for the proper selection of patients for short-term treatment and for the decision not to treat when there is significant character pathology. Where borderline or narcissistic issues prevail, they are more than likely to dominate the transference. Just as immature or pathological character structure will interfere with the resolution of the Oedipus complex developmentally, so it will interfere in treatment focusing on oedipal issues. As stated earlier, the successful completion of the separation-individuation process dovetails with the resolution of the Oedipus complex, with both coming about as the result of identificatory processes.

Shapiro (1979, p. 559) writes:

> The Oedipus complex is presented as a universal, developmentally determined mental organization that incorporates pregenital factors in a new hierarchic structure.

He says further:

> with maturation there is a discontinuous hierarchic organization such that structuralization at each stage reorganizes the mnemic traces of the prior stages. Thus, the oedipal constellation may supersede earlier experiences rendering them less 'toxic' than their previous level might suggest (p. 565).

He minimizes the impact of severe character pathology, saying that its only effect is to make oedipal themes more intense, more rigid, and more externally unstable.

Shapiro says, in effect, that the pregenital character is assimilated into and transformed by the Oedipus complex. In my experience with character disorders I have observed that quite the reverse is often true—that oedipal issues are assimilated into and transformed by preoedipal themes. In some instances the deficit of structure abort the development of the Oedipus complex. Competitive dynamics are assimilated into a dyadic structure rather than into a truly triangular one in which both "others" are of equal emotional significance. The oedipal situation is, by definition, triangular. It requires a mother who is sufficiently differentiated from the self and a father who is sufficiently differentiated from mother. The following is from the session of a young woman who presents with borderline lack of differentiation from the primary object, alongside a schizoid self.

Recently when I've called my parents, I didn't make any effort to chat any more. I'm taking the offensive of what my father does. He always says, 'Talk to mother.' Now I just say, 'Hi, where's Mommy?' I have a sense that my struggles are with my mother. I feel they exclude my father. In my mind I'm saying, 'Wait your turn. I want to work all this out with mother.' In a way, thinking of them separately seems a big change. To separate them and think of them in relation to me is very different. In the past I've been conscious of my mother's relationship with me. My father was lumped onto the side. Now the picture I get is one of an equilateral triangle, but the focus is on my mother. I don't consider the other (Horner 1979, 1984).

Her father's historical failure was that of failing to be available in a way that would have supported and even enabled her separation from mother. Her failure to differentiate herself from her mother was paralleled by her failure to differentiate mother from father. "My father was lumped onto the side." The Oedipus complex requires three separately perceived people and that the third element has some significant relational meaning for the individual. Sibling rivalry is triangular, but not oedipal. As a result of the young woman's analytic work, which focused on the issue of differentiation and boundary structuring, she approached the possibility of a true oedipal situation.

I have also worked with patients who presented with pseudo-triangular conflicts that appeared oedipal at first glance. However, they were situations in which object splitting was acted out with a separate good, idealized object, and a bad, persecutory object. The demand is often made of the "designated good object" (Horner 1979, 1984) to comfort when hurt by the bad one, and to "validate" the anger experienced toward the bad object so that the anger is good and righteous rather than the bad and dangerous rage of the infantile self. I refer to this as the "masochistic triangle" (p. 174). The idealized, omnipotent, good object representation is projected onto one parent, while the other parent is experienced as the all bad, persecuting object. That is, oedipal strivings are assimilated into the split self and object representational situation, and narcissistic issues become intensely sexualized. Transferences with these patients are particularly intractable.

In our work with short-term patients we have developed certain criteria that would enable the diagnostic distinctions that are critical: Are the major issues oedipal or preoedipal? Will the character structure lend itself to this treatment approach? These criteria are further elaborated in Chapters 5 and 6.

The achievement of our goals — the resolution of the Oedipus complex and its attendant conflicts — in short-term treatment depends on an appropriate selection of patients, on a thorough understanding of the issues involved, and on an assiduous attention to the maintenance of focus lest we find ourselves drawn retrogressively into preoedipal issues.

We attempt, in our work, to condense the uncovering, the working through, and the resolution of the oedipal issues into a maximum of 40 sessions, although, as Loewald notes, resolution is not necessarily obvious at the point of actual termination. As a phase of treatment, resolution is likely only to show its beginnings. Long-term follow-up will tell us if the goals have actually been achieved. Nevertheless, some changes in behavior and attitude should still be evident at the conclusion of our work.

In the following chapters the stages of treatment of oedipal issues in short-term therapy are explored in depth.

References

Blos, P. (1984). Son and father. *Journal of the American Psychoanalytic Association* 32:301–324.

Bromberg, P. (1983). The mirror and the mask: on narcissism and psychoanalytic growth. *Contemporary Psychoanalysis* 19:359–387.

Burgner, M., and Edgcumbe, R. (1972). Some problems in the conceptualization of early object relationships. Part II: the concept of object constancy. *Psychoanalytic Study of the Child* 27:315–333.

Davanloo, H. (1980). *Short-Term Dynamic Psychotherapy*. New York: Jason Aronson.

Freud, S. (1913). Totem and taboo: the horror of incest. *Standard Edition* 13:1–17.

_____. (1917a). The development of the libido and the sexual or-
ganizations. *Standard Edition* 16:320–338.

_____. (1917b). Introductory lectures on psycho-analysis: the libido
theory and narcissism. *Standard Edition* 16:412–430.

_____. (1921). Group psychology and the analysis of the ego: iden-
tification. *Standard Edition* 18:105–110.

_____. (1923). The ego and the id. *Standard Edition* 19:1–66.

_____. (1924). The dissolution of the Oedipus complex. *Standard
Edition* 19:172–179.

_____. (1931). Female sexuality. *Standard Edition* 21:223–243.

_____. (1933). New introductory lectures on psycho-analysis: the
dissection of the psychical personality. *Standard Edition* 22:57–
80.

Giovacchini, P. (1979). *Treatment of Primitive Mental States*. New
York: Jason Aronson.

Greenson, R. (1968). Disidentifying from mother: its special importance for the boy. In *Explorations in Psychoanalysis*, pp. 305–
312. New York: International Universities Press.

Horner, A. (1979, 1984). *Object Relations and the Developing Ego
in Therapy*, 1st and 2nd eds. New York: Jason Aronson.

_____. (1980). The roots of anxiety, character structure, and psy-
choanalytic treatment. *Journal of the American Academy of
Psychoanalysis* 8:565–573.

Loewald, H. W. (1979). The waning of the Oedipus complex. *Journal of the American Psychoanalytic Association* 27:751–775.

Mahler, M., Pine, F., and Bergman, A. (1975). *The Psychological
Birth of the Human Infant*. New York: Basic Books.

Sandler, J., Holder, A., and Meers, D. (1963). The ego ideal and
the ideal self. *Psychoanalytic Study of the Child* 18:139–158.

Schecter, D. (1968). Identification and individuation. *Journal of the
American Psychoanalytic Association* 16:48–80.

Shapiro, T. (1977). Oedipal distortions in severe character pathol-
ogies: developmental and theoretical considerations. *Psychoanalytic Quarterly* 46:555–579.

Tolpin, M. (1971). On the beginnings of a cohesive self: an application of the concept of transmuting internalization to the study
of the transitional object in signal anxiety. *Psychoanalytic Study
of the Child* 26:316–352.

Chapter 3

PROBLEMS OF TECHNIQUE
VICTOR GOLDIN, M.D.

Need for Systematic Guidelines

Those readers who are considering the eventual applications of the techniques herein to practice would do well to acknowledge in themselves elements of cynicism. Veterans of psychotherapeutic practice have lived through many fads that heralded great promise and then faded. The scars borne by early enthusiasms turned into disappointments heal painfully.

If the reader can suspend his disbelief, a reminder is in order: Practice and systematic attention to detail are fundamental to learning any new skill. Short-term therapy based on psychoanalysis seems so familiar that there is a tendency to rush off equipped with one's comfortable therapeutic style and find, with dismay, "there's nothing really new here." This is erroneous. The techniques are similar, but the differences are critical.

The section on supervision in this Chapter addresses itself to the effort necessary to begin a systematic practice of short-term psychotherapy.

Case Example: Understanding the Terrain. The following introduces the case of Alice D.

As the 33-year-old certified public accountant walked down the corridor to begin her third short-term psychotherapy session, Alice D.'s tailored navy blue skirt constrained her stride. The effect was not unlike the mask of perfect composure that she had worn to the first interview a month ago.

Dr. Andrew R. once again began to peel away the layers of generalities with which the sessions always began. His meticulous attention to detail had been rewarded by seeing the patient who sat before him change from a premature spinster to a betrayed 12-year-old whose father had just divorced his wife and left his three daughters. Alice, the most vivacious of the girls, knew she was her father's favorite just as she "knew" she was the "most intelligent" woman in the family. She had burned with indignation at what she perceived as her father's desertion of her. Like an Olympian: lofty and superior, she stood abandoned and exposed, poised to receive the victor's crown, which never touched her head. From that point of life on, that pose became her posture. Head up, self-contained, superior to those around her, Alice carried the look of one who had beaten them all. Only a life of near total absence of joy revealed the farce.

Alice was admitted to therapy with complaints about the paucity of men, with dissatisfaction over her job, and with a fear that life had passed her by.

"He's not there for me," she explained when quizzed about the specifics of her feelings toward 50-year-old Sy. Pressed again and again the bitterness slowly surfaced. Warding off distracting details, Dr. R. exposed Alice's sense of betrayal, probed for resentment toward other women, and made his silent assessment.

Minutes later Alice was talking of her father and his "midlife crisis" 20 years earlier. Again Dr. R. pushed for details and was rewarded with an outburst of tearful recriminations. The measure of experienced betrayal was gauged and marked, and exploration into feelings about mother and siblings rounded out this area.

These inquiries, and others like them, had given

Dr. R. the necessary details for charting the course of treatment.

Some Principles of Treatment

Treatment in psychotherapy can be likened to a well-planned journey. As with all journeys, a map must first be drawn with starting point and ending destination. There must be a sense of where one wishes to help a patient go, a clear view of where one is, and what yet must be dealt with. And knowledge of the interrelation of the major people in the patient's past and current life will help the therapist guide the patient to journey's end.

DYNAMIC ACTIVITY LEVEL IS ESSENTIAL

Short-term therapy requires an activity level that is alien to psychoanalytic psychotherapists. In the pioneering days when unconscious processes were being discovered, warnings against wild analyses were correctly raised. Psychoanalysis was recognized not only as a therapeutic modality, but also as a general theory of human behavior. Each analysis, carefully and correctly performed, provided new material in the unfolding exploration of the human psyche. One learned to listen "with a third ear" to the marvelously complex and rich tapestry. The importance of patient's resistances and working with them only gradually became part of the therapist's armamentarium.

Careful, cautious, and conservative therapists, however, increasingly hesitated to distort and deflect free associations. Over the years, the tempo of therapist intervention slowed, and generations of therapists adopted an "analytic stance," which often meant more silence and fewer interventions.

Short-term dynamic psychotherapy demands a taxing alertness, attention to fundamentals of resistance and transference, and the courage to intervene built on a conviction and a knowledge of what is going on between patient and therapist.

Provocative research by Malan (1976) implies that more active intervention by therapists brings about greater change. Although these findings, like so much in psychotherapy, await controlled and systematic research, we feel they are valid.

Short-term dynamic psychotherapy when well conducted does not contain long periods of silence by the therapist. It demands, instead, quick zeroing in on the sessions' adaptive context* and the reading of the material in the light of that context. Agility is demanded, with the therapist prepared to make a move quickly.

Denied the luxury of endless hours of "hovering attention," the therapist must listen actively, judge the impact of his remarks, measure resistances, and move again.

Stalemates are circumvented; diversions by the patient are challenged or otherwise overcome. Flat, affectless hours are not tolerated.

Case Example: Using the Adaptive Context. The following illustrates the use of the adaptive context, which refers to the manner in which patients handle their core neurotic conflicts as they present in everyday life events, and the need for the therapist to focus actively.

> As the third session began, Alice D. casually remarked that she had overheard the receptionist talking with a coworker about the department moving to a new building. With only a few more clues, Dr. R. decided that this represented the adaptive context. Forearmed, he focused on her feelings that he might somehow move away. "Yes," she acknowledged this had been a tangential thought but she'd felt that it was "too silly" to mention. The therapist maintained the focus on her feelings of abandonment and betrayal and wove them back and forth between those feelings directed toward him and similar feelings toward her father. The therapist felt that since Alice's anger and

---

Editor's note: Langs (1976) defines "the adaptive context" as the "main event — inner and outer experience — that the patient is adjusting and responding to . . . " (p. 9). This may be an announcement of the therapist's vacation or a change in the time of the appointment by the therapist. It may be the patient's report of his failure to be promoted at work. Whatever the event, it has unconscious implications that will, in some way, relate to the therapeutic focus, including the transference.

jealousy toward her mother had seemed less than in other oedipal dramas, he could safely omit much probing of feelings toward the "other women."

OEDIPAL FOCUS MUST BE MAINTAINED

Dynamic core issues must be kept in mind at all times. Preoedipal issues exist in all patients, but the therapist should not be diverted by this material. It is the resolution of oedipal conflicts that provides the energy for reparative growth.

In any given interchange, an admixture of characterologic issues and pre- and postoedipal issues can be discerned. Characterologic issues are approached if they constitute resistances; preoedipal considerations are most often laid aside. Oedipal issues become the focus of the therapist's attention.

The therapist's principal task is to maintain this focus; it cannot be left to chance or to the patient. Guided back to the core issues, appropriate patients will move ahead with gratifying rapidity.

Case Example: The Oedipal Material. Although preoedipal material is almost always available, the therapist concentrates on the oedipal material when possible.

ALICE D.: I remember my father but vaguely, somehow.

DR. R.: Tell me about him.

ALICE D.: He was a very important lawyer.

DR. R.: How did you address him?

ALICE D.: I don't know what you mean.

DR. R.: When you were 12, before he left, you called him "daddy," "pops," what?

ALICE D.: "poppa." It was my special name; it had such a soft cuddly sound.

DR. R.: It was *your* special name for him.

ALICE D.: I had rights; I'd nestle up in his lap and smell his pipe.

DR. R.: But Gwen [younger sister] was in the way of your special rights.

ALICE D.:   For a long time I just seemed . . . I don't know
            . . . to ignore her. I would just think of coming
            into the den, the fire crackling. I'd like to tell him
            what I'd done in school. He seemed so accepting
            . . . he was so warm . . . like a big jolly sun . . .
            all over.

DR. R.:   So you got rid of Gwen.

ALICE D.:   No, I just didn't seem to notice . . . she was shy.

DR. R.:   She's out of your picture.

ALICE D.:   I had a lot of warm feelings . . . poppa feelings.

DR. R.:   Gwen would interfere.

ALICE D.:   She liked mother better.

DR. R.:   But you pushed her out.

ALICE D.:   That's a way of putting it, I guess.

DR. R.:   You say, "I guess," but you did want her out of
            the picture. . . .

TRANSFERENCE NOT TO BE AVOIDED

Transference, as used here, is a concept broadened in a manner most
recently delineated by Gill (1982). The therapist's active effort to
see himself as an actor in all of the unfolding dramas is not to be
avoided. The therapist, who has his own narcissism well in hand,
will not avoid the transferential hints and implications embodied
in almost every aspect of every session. Such tenacious attention to
the role of the therapist may strike some as arrogant and ill-
conceived, but we have found that the contrary is true. Patients are
not adversely affected by this preoccupation on the part of the
therapist. More often than not, such courageous and bold thinking strengthens the therapeutic alliance and saves endless hours. Patients are not forced to struggle with half-experienced and tentatively
expressed attitudes toward the therapist. Many therapists are reticent
to come to grips with negative views of themselves. Such feelings
often sit atop genuine tender feelings that cannot be experienced with
true affect until the negative attitudes are expressed openly.
    Attention must be paid to the therapist's feelings generated by

the interaction. Countertransference must be appreciated constantly. The supervisory process and solo video replay (see below) are invaluable in sensitizing the therapist to his ongoing inner experience. Here, as in so many other technical considerations, activity on the part of the therapist is crucial. Vague, ill-defined feelings must be concentrated on by the therapist to bring into sharp focus the specific interaction that is taking place. The illumination and detail that this process produces help steer a course along the therapeutic map.

Case Example: Transference. This is a vignette from the fifth session that illustrates how the transference issues are exploited.

ALICE D.: There is something about him [Sy, current man friend] that turns me off.

DR. R.: Something about him?

ALICE D.: I don't know, sloppiness.

DR. R.: Tell me about sloppiness.

ALICE D.: Just the way he keeps himself, messy I guess.

DR. R.: Messy . . . something messy. . . . You have feeling about it?

ALICE D.: I don't know, I'm neat he's messy.

DR. R.: Messy?

ALICE D.: Things all over.

DR. R.: Hmmm . . . Sy's messy.

ALICE D.: He's a slob.

DR. R.: Sy's messy . . . a slob . . . it bothers you. What bothers you?

ALICE D.: I don't know . . . it's embarrassing.

DR. R.: You know but you say you don't know.

ALICE D.: The smell . . . it's hard to talk about it.

DR. R.: The smell?

ALICE D.: Yes, it's odd . . . it was his aftershave that I used to like so much . . . now I've changed.

DR. R.: Now it's different? Sy's smell.

ALICE D.: It's worse in the afternoon, but I can't blame him.

DR. R.:   Smell is worse in the afternoon.

ALICE D.:   It's like body odor. . . . He comes from work
            and he has sweated and dried and sweated. . . .
            It's musty, acrid.

DR. R.:   Men who've sweated by late in the day, you have
            feeling about that.

ALICE D.:   Not men . . . I'm talking about Sy.

DR. R.:   Yes, I know. You are talking about Sy and he's
            sloppy and he smells . . . but other men.

ALICE D.:   I never tell them, it would hurt too much.

DR. R.:   You wouldn't want to hurt men.

ALICE D.:   That's right, it would embarrass them.

DR. R.:   Telling a man that he's sloppy, that he's messy
            . . . that he smelled in the afternoon, would em-
            barrass, hurt the man.

ALICE D.:   That's right, I wouldn't like to see the pain.

DR. R.:   We meet in the afternoon.

ALICE D.:   Yes, so?

DR. R.:   You have some feelings about my being neat or
            sloppy?

ALICE D.:   Well that's a hard one.

DR. R.:   That's a hard one? Why a hard one?

ALICE D.:   Well . . . your office isn't exactly the neatest.

DR. R.:   My office . . . We are talking about me not my
            office.

ALICE D.:   It's hard to say.

DR. R.:   Something is hard to say?

ALICE D.:   It's hard to come right out . . . but I have noticed
            your desk is untidy.

DR. R.:   Untidy . . . Sy is messy and a slob, and my desk
            is "untidy."

ALICE D.:   Okay, messy. I'm sorry, but your desk is messy.

DR. R.:   You're *sorry* . . . my desk is messy.

ALICE D.:   I'm sorry to be so blunt.

DR. R.:   You don't want to be blunt with me. How about the smell? You're hedging there, too?

ALICE D.:   This *really* is hard. Okay . . . you have a smell. BO at times. I try to ignore it but I can't get it out of my mind. I know it's 4:30, you've been racing around all day, but it's close in here. The smell . . . I can't ignore it. It touches everything. I really am very nervous talking this way. . . .

DR. R.:   Nervous telling me about my smell?

INTERVENTION ADVANCES THERAPY

Each intervention by the therapist must have purpose and meaning. The therapist should be able to understand and identify every intervention, and although some comments and questions can serve the purpose of clarification, they are minimal. Most interventions are part of a process of gradually building toward therapeutic insight. Steps should be simple and orderly. Techniques include tentative suggestions that the patient is asked to consider. The therapist will frequently point to an interaction, which has occurred within the therapeutic hour, and get the patient's acknowledgment of what has transpired. For example: "You are deferring to me again, to placate me. What is going on?" This is used as a building block to similar interactions with other people in current life and in the past. Again and again this is woven back into the initially delineated core dynamics. Therapists should not be afraid of simple statements. All individuals learn slowly, and patients are best helped with several short, easily understood, and moderately repetitive statements. Long, intellectually convoluted, theoretically correct, but difficult to understand statements are avoided. Patients do not depreciate a therapist's efforts as "too simplistic." Where a patient so labels an intervention, it is most often a sign of resistance and to be worked as such. One might reply, "By labeling what I say as simplistic, you divert us from looking at the issue."

Motivational comments are frequently in order. When the resistance is imbedded in the patient's passivity, the patient must be helped to take responsibility for his life. The therapist will find many times and many opportunities, with most patients, to "throw the ball into his court." The patient must truly appreciate his stake in the success of therapy. Any opportunity that the patient takes to adopt a passive role and wait for magical repair will prove detrimental to therapy.

P: I don't know why I do that.

T: What is your hunch about it?

It is the tone of the interventions, relying on the mature and healthy aspects of the patient's personality, that advances the therapy toward a more rapid and successful conclusion.

The Use of Video Equipment in the Course of Treatment

Success in short-term therapy is significantly dependent on appropriate supervision and review. No therapist, no matter how well trained, can undertake this work without spending extensive time and effort in perfecting the technique. It is paradoxical, but true, that the very brevity of treatment, so beneficial to the patient, is purchased with extra time and effort invested by the therapist.

We have found that the use of video equipment is essential. Nothing can provide the therapist with so complete and undistorted a review of his work.

The equipment needed to provide useful records for supervision and "self-vision" is inexpensive, unobtrusive, and easily available. We have found that a ½-inch format is well adapted to our needs. The ½-inch tape is inexpensive, particularly when recorded on the 6-hour mode, and the consumer recording deck is universally available. A sensitive color video camera, with a built-in digital timer can be purchased for about $1,000. We recommend high-fidelity microphones and a microphone mixer.

The most important feature of the equipment is its simplicity. Before each session the therapist should have the equipment ready so that he turns on only a few switches and makes a minimum number of adjustments. There is no need to further attend to the equipment once the session begins.

The technical elements that form the bedrock of short-term

therapy are the focus of supervision whether done by the practitioner alone, with the aid of a colleague, or (in the best of circumstances) both alone and with a supervisor. Self-supervision is a process requiring great discipline. Here, the video recording, bringing life to previously held sessions, can be invaluable. The time demanded for such "extra" supervision is a real consideration. Video decks are so readily available that if the patient's confidentiality can be carefully maintained, reviewing at home is possible. Although viewing one's own work without a colleague cannot remove some blind spots, such efforts, if done often enough, will bear fruit.

Sensitivity to unconscious processes should be constantly reinforced. Those therapists who have the discipline to review a taped session several times are always rewarded by the subtle revelations that leap from the screen on the third and fourth viewing. If this review is done close to the next session, the therapist comes with his mind "rubbed raw." He is alert and actively prepared to listen to transference implications, clues to linkages to the core neurotic problems, and potential resistances.

In review, one listens to the adaptive context. How quickly and successfully was it grasped? One listens to interventions. Were they delayed? Could they have been made more promptly? Has the patient been allowed to ramble? Were diversionary meanderings permitted to develop?

Therapists making the transition from a more leisurely mode to an anxiety-provoking active style can reward themselves with the time to reflect. Unconscious clues to transference and dynamics will make themselves apparent without the distraction of patient or supervisor. All of the technical points addressed in the following case example in terms of supervision are applicable in self-supervision as well.

Case Example. As illustrated in this selection from the 11th session, supervision can help with countertransference issues that have been overlooked by the therapist.

Alice D. discussed the long arguments she'd had with her father. Excitement seemed part of it. They'd argue well past midnight. Mother would go to bed. The yelling and the tears [on her part] would go on until finally he would

apologize. It was a delicious moment. The glow of recon-
ciliation and then the exhausted relief.

DR. R.:   You fought with your father?

ALICE D.: Not fought, argued.

DR. R.:   But really you fought.

ALICE D.: They weren't fights, they were arguments.

The session went back and forth with much hair splitting. On
review in supervision, the fact that the therapist had gotten stuck
at this point became evident. It then became clear to him that the
scenes described paralleled his interaction with his own daughter,
Barbara. Those nights when neither father nor daughter could let
go were being relived.

Supervision: An Integral Part of Therapy

Time spent in supervision has an inverse relationship to the length
of therapy. As practiced by our group at Beth Israel Medical Center,
the number of hours spent in reviewing the material of therapy far
exceeds the amount of time that would be spent in reviewing a similar
treatment by a supervisory analyst in a psychoanalytic training institute. A minimum of one supervisory hour should be spent for each
therapeutic hour. It is anticipated that as facility develops, it will
be possible to reduce the enormous expenditure of time involved.
However, therapists who desire to work in short-time therapy, as
presented in this volume, should be prepared to obtain supervision
for themselves and to spend considerable time in perfecting their
technique.

Given these time commitments, it is expensive for the private
practitioner to devote the necessary time to supervision. Supervision
of the first dozen cases, in the meticulous fashion recommended,
is best seen as an investment in advanced training. With a model
of continuing professional commitment to training in mind, the
therapist who finds excitement and gratification in short-term therapy will be willing to pay the price. Patients told that their therapy
may take from 20 to 30 sessions are often willing to pay a slightly

higher fee, as they are able to anticipate the total cost of therapy. Patients also appreciate the additional cost that video recordings and supervision entails.

Supervision has taken on the coloring of its pedagogical roots and usually refers to the student (lower, novice, neophyte) and the teacher (higher, expert, guru). Although this is a true picture of things in a variety of settings in which psychotherapy is taught, it is an unfortunate model that should be broken.

Because short-term therapy has appeal for therapists who have been in practice for many years and because we rely heavily on video records, a number of our senior colleagues are asked to expose their work. Although all have done so in student days, doing so after arriving at professional heights raises new problems. The fear of exposure often increases with years of practice. Because of this fear we have tried to establish a "supervisory alliance." This refers to the mutual, mature, cooperative effort in overseeing therapy. As with the "therapeutic alliance" (important in the extreme in short-term therapy), the participants have specialized tasks. Just as in therapy the patient knows the details of his life and story and the analyst knows how to go about analysis; in the best of circumstances, the two join forces on a common mission. This is what we hope to achieve in supervision. Our core group, at Beth Israel Medical Center, has been able to develop that mutual trust and sensitivity that has made the exposure of one's work an adventure rather than a threat. It is our conviction that most therapists and colleagues can establish such a relationship. Our work with two outstanding therapists in the field, Drs. Peter Sifneos and Habib Davanloo, have encouraged us in this belief.

The supervisory process should be directed toward maintenance of the therapeutic focus. All therapists are, by the nature of psychotherapeutic interaction, constantly being diverted.

In brief therapy a focus, often oedipal, is delineated at the time of the initial evaluation. It is important that the therapist have the focus clearly in mind. Supervisors can help ensure that the therapy does not get underway without an agreed upon plan of where the therapeutic territory is located. This does not mean that the entire map of the trip can be anticipated, but it does mean that the therapist be helped in making a commitment about the basic dynamics that are involved in the maladaptive symptoms for which the patient seeks help. The supervisor or supervisory group insists on formulating the areas of disturbance and the neurotic core. Vague, fuzzy dynamics are not permitted. Therapists who have enjoyed the luxury of "letting the material unfold" find it difficult to formulate and then commit to working in the areas outlined.

We have found that the careful initial evaluation can uncover the core neurosis. Therapists and supervisors are well advised to commit the formulation to paper. This practice, which may seem simplistic to seasoned therapists, nevertheless has proved its worth. Since the therapists who are learning this new technique will include senior staff as well as trainees, insistence on this for all is especially important.

Organizational structure is often turned on its head when an entire department or group of clinicians are trying to understand and utilize a technique that, although based on Freudian psychoanalytic principles, is radically different in some of its applications. Unless there is rigid adherence to the rule, senior analysts might be "excused" from writing their formulations and committing to paper a statement of the core neurosis. This will, we believe, prove to be a mistake. Once the supervisor(s) and the therapist have agreed on the therapeutic focus, the job is to help the therapist stay as close as possible to that focus.

It is here that the trip becomes potentially rocky. The supervisory process has to contend with the patient's efforts to divert the therapy from its main track. The resistances that the patient manifests will in no way be different from the resistances seen in psychoanalytically oriented therapy endeavors. These must be dealt with vigorously. In addition, the supervisor has to deal with the therapist's tendencies to deviate. All who have supervised psychoanalytic therapy appreciate the myriad issues involved. Not only are there the well-known countertransference problems (see below), and not only do we have errors that arise from lack of clear dynamic thinking, as in any supervision, but we have the additional problem of errors that are made because the therapist is too seasoned.

The "too seasoned" therapist automatically returns to treating patients in short-term therapy as he would treat any patient in psychotherapy. The therapist, by habit, reverts to his or her old way of practicing psychotherapy. It is understandable how these errors arise. The therapist is, after all, facing a patient who talks the same, at least initially, as other psychotherapy patients. More often than not, this return to previous therapeutic strategies involves passivity on the part of the therapist. Trained in the psychoanalytic model, the therapist has learned to hold his fire until he is sure of his material. He spends extra time listening to make sure he understands the issue of the hour in the greatest possible detail.

Then there is a drift toward preoedipal material. Short-term therapy can usually be accomplished with patients where analysis of their preoedipal content is not essential. It is difficult for many therapists without supervision to steer a course that avoids getting caught in the shoals of preoedipal material.

TRANSFERENCE

Transference is handled in short-term therapies with an immediacy that demands constant attention. All therapists profit from having a third party help them pick up early transference implications in the material. The role of the supervisor is to help the therapist see manifestations of transference early. Video-recorded sessions are excellent for this purpose. Nonverbal clues are available to the supervisor or supervisory group to add to the verbal material. Because it is so important in short-term therapy to handle the transference issues as early as possible, a therapist is best served who has an alert supervisor and who has the advantage of looking at films and hearing the subtleties of language, voice, and tone.

"How perceptive of you," the patient, a business school graduate, said to the therapist. The therapist did not pick up on the comment. Only in watching the body posture (arrogantly erect) and in hearing the snide tones of the patient was it vividly clear in supervision that the patient's negative transference reactions had not been confronted. The competitiveness and hostility behind such a comment will prove to be issues central to the core issues.

It is essential in short-term therapy that a transference neurosis not be permitted to develop. Early identification of transference manifestations are invaluable in aborting a transference neurosis. Comments made in the waiting room, out of the recorder's hearing, or as the patient goes out the door, are often heavy with implications. The supervisory task of pointing out opportunities, seized and missed, for therapist/patient linkages is an endless one. It gives the therapist additional eyes and ears in finding transference opportunities and helps keep the transference issue "alive."

The problem of handling resistance in short-term therapy is of singular importance. Discussions with the supervisor about which resistances are actually impeding progress is of great help to the therapist.

As in supervision of all dynamic psychoanalytically oriented psychotherapy, there are times when the patient's resistance is missed by the therapist. Indeed, in classical analysis this can happen for some time. There may be sessions that are "dry," and long periods may go by before the fact of a massive resistance is realized by therapist and supervisor alike. As mentioned above, as an example of transference (arrogant, erect, business school graduate), the videotape supplies additional clues to resistance. The patient's posture, tone of voice, as well as content of speech, all have messages. Working quickly, a therapist has time to sit back with a helpful colleague and contemplate the innumerable bits and byplays that are taking place rapidly during the unfolding 50-minute session. It sometimes happens that one comes across resistances serendipitously. Such an occasion presented itself when therapist and patient were off camera at the end of a session and caught by the microphone as they discussed the patient's fee. The overhearing provided the supervisory group with new material to help the therapist, who failed to recognize the important message in the patient's handling of the fee. Helplessness and powerlessness as a defensive posture may be hidden in complaints about money, as may resentment of the power of the therapist to collect the fee.

Omissions are another fertile source for recognizing resistance. The supervisor, fresh to the case after a week's absence, and protected from the heavy emotional bombardment of the session, is often much better able than the therapist to note how material from one session, or one part of a session, has been omitted or sidetracked.

COUNTERTRANSFERENCE

Since one hour of supervision is recommended for each hour of therapy, it is possible to spend time helping the therapist connect with his or her inner feelings. Here again the video provides a valuable tool in helping the therapist acknowledge to him/herself the boredom that may be apparent on the screen, or the bodily movements that depict annoyance, frustration, sexual excitement, contempt, dismay, or perplexity.

FOCUS

Although already mentioned, this critical issue needs reiteration. The supervisor can relentlessly assist the therapist in sticking to an agreed upon work path. An element rarely mentioned in this regard is simply the installation of courage. Working with a patient is lonely business. The therapist often has only slim clues to guide him on his path. The patient, sometimes, but not always, a cooperative fellow, is often busy denying and depreciating the little rocks and ridges that the therapist is using to guide him toward the goal of better psychic health. The supervisory process gives the therapist the validation he may need to push on in the face of the bleakness of the landscape and the negation of the patient. The supervisor sees the sense in what the therapist is trying to do and encourages him when the going gets rough.

SPECIFICITY

In a therapy session a patient confessed, with heightened effect, how he had seen his mother in the bath by looking through a crack in the bathroom door. The supervisor encouraged the therapist to ask for details about what he saw. The therapist was reluctant to press for details and resisted the supervisor's suggestion that these would be helpful. The therapist explored his reservations with the supervisor. There were countertransferential issues. He had some aggressive feelings toward the patient which he did not recognize except as they came out in his "not wanting to hurt" the patient. In addition, the therapist realized that he was warding off his own voyeuristic impulses. Fortified by the supervisory work, the therapist at the next opportunity did indeed find that the mother had "pendulous breasts with very large and spread nipples." This material proved to be valuable some weeks later when remembering and encouraged by the previous supervision, the therapist was able to obtain a description of the patient's wife. To a "T" her breasts were described by the patient as having exactly the same contour and coloration as the patient's mother's. This allowed for an important dynamic linkage. There are numerous times in supervision when the therapist can be encouraged to go after details. Therapists trained in more passive expectant waiting have to be constantly reminded of the value of uncovering hidden fantasies by going after minute concrete detail.

The Rule of Abstinence. The analytic prohibition first suggested by Freud (1912) against gratification of unconscious wishes is important in this work. Because the therapist is active, there is danger that this stimulus to the unconscious process will not be fully utilized. Supervision showing the therapist's face as smiling, nodding, as well as his comments, help check an inclination toward overgratification, or toward an unconscious collusion to avoid underlying negative feelings or anxiety.

Appendix: A Postscript on Video Taping

It should be clear that video recordings help to maintain the supervisory track. They enable one to check on the working alliance, find clues to the early development of transference outcroppings, and note physical clues that may indicate resistances of all kind and harbingers of incipient acting out. They also are useful as a check on the therapist's ability to clarify and confront, and they assist in unearthing hidden countertransferential difficulties, searching out violations of the rule of abstinence.

Thus, all of the important aspects of short-term therapy and supervision are aided by the use of modern video recordings. In addition, video records prove invaluable for research and have special value in outcome research. Six-month, 1-year, and 5-year follow-ups in which the patient is carefully led back over the areas of disturbance will help settle whether psychotherapy works and whether its results are long-lasting. The virtues of video recording are the same for all types of psychotherapy but have special relevance for short-term work. In classical psychoanalysis it is obvious that the sheer mass of material collected day after day makes minute supervision physically impossible. Research into the psychotherapeutic situation is also hampered in that there is too much stored on tape to be systematically viewed. Efforts to use computers to help organize linguistic or other data have promise for segments of the process but also have inherent difficulties. Short-term dynamic therapy lasts for an average of 20 hours and can be supervised and studied minutely. Although that amount of material is admittedly large, it is manageable enough to help put psychotherapy into the mainstream of scientific activity.

Despite all of the above, many therapists find the concept of using video equipment unacceptable. There are a number of reasons advanced for these feelings. We have found few difficulties in using and maintaining equipment and feel that any therapist or therapeutic center that plans on using short-term dynamic therapy should most seriously consider the equipment as a sine qua non for doing this kind of work in a professionally responsible manner. It goes without saying that there are unconscious reasons that make many therapists object to the use of the equipment. These must be addressed by the individual therapist. They may find that their own fear of exposure is among the main stumbling blocks to the use of video recordings. Other issues to consider are warded off exhibitionistic conflicts and excessively rigid concerns about the potential harm to patients. Similarly, although obviously no patient should be coerced into accepting taping of sessions, it is often worth speculating about patients who refuse. It often happens that patients who refuse come to reveal, after a few sessions, the pathology behind their refusal. An ethical question arises, if the center feels as we do, that adequate supervision requires the use of video recordings. Can anyone be treated without video? We are coming to the position that when confronted with a patient who cannot, for whatever reason, accept the video taping, we do not treat them in short-term therapy. Naturally, since we treat a number of professionals, including physicians and their families, we are careful to explain that care will be taken to ensure that films are not shown for educational purposes in an area where the patient is likely to be recognized.

After all of the above discussion of the resistance to the use of video recording by therapists and patients, we find that, in fact, very few patients refuse. It has been our experience that if staff groups working together trust each other, and if the situation is explained in a "matter of fact" manner, there is little opposition. With the patients we take the position that video recording is a modern, more complete, and more sophisticated kind of note taking.

References

Freud, S. (1912). Recommendations to physicians practicing psycho-analysis. *Standard Edition* 12:111–120. London: Hogart.

Gill, M. M. (1982). *Analysis of Transference.* Vol I: *Theory and Technique. Psychological Issues.* Monograph 53.

Langs, R. J. (1976). *The Therapeutic Interaction.* New York: Jason Aronson.

Malan, D. H. (1976). *The Frontier of Brief Psychotherapy.* New York: Plenum Press.

Editor's note: Although the use of video equipment adds tremendously to the effectiveness of training and self-supervision, the practitioner should not be deterred from undertaking this form of treatment in its absence. There is no doubt that maximum information will be derived from the use of the camera. For example, the erotic component of the transference may be missed if one does not note the seductive posture. Nevertheless, the use of good audio equipment with reporting of nonverbal behaviors can and have been effective in the learning process. Once the technique has been relatively well mastered, the process of ongoing self-supervision can be carried out with the use of verbatim notes. Although there may be some disagreement on this point, this has been my own experience. The notes are reviewed methodically before *every* session throughout treatment, to ensure fidelity to the basic principles of brief therapy.

Chapter 4

PRINCIPLES FOR THE THERAPIST

ALTHEA J. HORNER, PH.D.

The principles of brief therapy aim for the prevention of a therapeutic style that would prolong treatment. Some of these principles are equally useful in long-term treatment, although their application would vary according to the therapist's belief as to what is useful with any given patient, irrespective of metapsychology.

The principles to be considered here are (1) activity, (2) clarity, (3) specificity, (4) immediacy, (5) interpreting upward, (6) maintaining the focus, (7) vigilant monitoring and interpretation of the transference, whether it be expressed directly or by allusion, and (8) interpreting the triads.

Activity

The therapist does not sit back and wait for the material to unfold, but from the very beginning is active in the maintenance of the focus, in the interpretation of the transference, and in the application of the other mechanics essential to time-limited treatment.

As therapy moves from the uncovering phase to the working-through phase, the therapist will be less and less active and the patient will take increasing responsibility, confronting his own defensive postures, such as passivity or vagueness. Indeed, by the end of treatment, if all transference resistances are dissolved, the patient will take active responsibility for the scheduling of termination.

The activity of the therapist is well illustrated by Dr. Been's exchange with the patient, bringing into focus the relationship between his reaction to his brother's birth and his reaction to his colleague at work.

T: So you sat outside the room, unnoticed and quiet.

P: Yes. My mother was so busy and happy taking care of Tim.

T: But what happened to your close relationship with her?

P: I don't know. I never thought about that.

T: How did you feel toward Tim?

P: I liked him very much. He was so cute and we are so close now.

T: So Tim arrived and occupied center stage with your mother.

P: That's true. But I accepted it. Occasionally I got jealous when he played with my toys. Once I hit him hard when he played with one of my toy soldiers.

T: So, it's clear you felt very angry when Tim played with something you wanted. Certainly not a passive response.

P: Yes, that's true. But aren't all kids that way?

T: So when Tim went into your mother's lap, that place you liked so much, you sat passively in the hall. I wonder how you felt.

P: I think you are stretching it.

T: So, how did you behave with your colleague John last weekend at the board meeting?

P: Well, I told you already I was passive! But I was burning inside. John knew that the boss was giving him points so he continued to show off.

T: So with John you were passive outside, but burning inside. Can't we say that you handled Tim's birth also by becoming passive and burning inside?

The dialogue is intense, with the active therapist making connections from a to b to c, with a cutting-through of the denial of the patient's resentments toward his baby brother, feelings and defenses against feelings that continue to be acted out in his present day life.

This high level of therapist activity, interpreting by making juxtapositions, linking the past with the present in and out of the treatment situations, maintains the focus and keeps the patient from going off in other directions which, though interesting, would work against the principles of brief treatment.

A 40-year-old man in middle management of a large corporation complaned of being unable to advance and of being passed over in promotions despite his high level of expertise. The defenses he used against taking power with its associated guilt and anxiety were being uncovered. His asking questions of the therapist was identified as a way to placate the authority figure, a way to deny his wish to challenge that authority. This first became evident in his manner with the therapist. He began to explore the ways he did this with his parents, with teachers, and with his superiors at work. Here he could only function from a position of dominance over his subordinates, or from a position of subservience with his seniors. In the working-through phase of treatment, when he would ask this kind of question, he would stop himself and say, "I must be trying to placate you." At this point the therapist asked, "What's going on now that you feel you have to placate me?" At this point, the patient is confronting himself, and exploration of the dynamics behind this defensive posture is undertaken. The resistance to the uncovering of these dynamics is minimal once the defensive posture itself is identified, labeled, and acknowledged. The therapist became less and less active as treatment progressed.

Clarity

The therapist should never assume she or he understands what the patient means if this meaning is not patently clear. Vagueness as a defense protects the patient from awareness of thoughts or feelings that would evoke anxiety. The defensive style itself is confronted with the simple statement, "you are being vague." This will most likely provoke some anxiety that may be connected with the therapist as a transference reaction, or that may be connected with the repressed material itself. Exploration of the dynamics behind the defense will be part of the therapeutic process.

Clarification is also indicated when the material presented is incomplete, being characterized by a narrative quality without the feelings or beliefs that were operative at the time of the event being reported. For example, one patient reported that two guys quit after he took over the job of supervisor. He also reported in the same detached manner the fact that he had to fire someone. Inquiry about the missing elements of the experience is indicated to clarify what was actually going on at the time that is relevant to the therapeutic focus. In this instance, the conflict about power and aggression would prove to be central to treatment.

The use of words that are assumed to have consensual meaning when it is more likely that they have specific meaning for the patient should be clarified. Words like "rejection" in particular lend themselves to this kind of obfuscation. What constitutes a rejection for this person? What is the fear? the fantasy? the reaction?

Indication of affect must be addressed, even though the patient communicates nonverbally, as with a smile. The inquiry into the feelings being experienced then leads to associations and memories that deepened the exploration and work of treatment. For example, when Dr. Been says, "Are you aware you're smiling?" the patient tells him about the memory that has evoked the smile.

Then, when the patient mentions a feeling but without much affect, inquiry into the patient's experience enables her to go deeper into the feelings, to experience them with greater intensity, and to reach some insight about those feelings.

Specificity

Global statements about the self, such as "I usually back down when someone disagrees with me," are unproductive and tend to be more ruminative than analytic. Asking for specific examples of times the person has backed down under such circumstances in his current life, such as at work or with parental figures, will enable full exploration of the dynamic. Instances of the occurrence of the dynamic in the treatment situation should be noted and explored.

It is easy to let generalizations slip by without recognizing them unless one is alert to this as an issue to be managed. Following are some examples:

P: I hide things.

T: Can you give me an example?

P: I'm afraid of feeling things.

T: Where does this show up? With whom in particular?

P: I could be more successful.

T: What holds you back?

P: I think I've been self-destructive.

T: Give me some examples.

P: I'm afraid of rejection.

T: What about it is distressing?

One might be fooled into thinking that the patient is dealing with important material when he makes such general statements as noted above. But they are probably things the patient has said about himself many times before without subjecting these statements to any kinds of exploration.

Vagueness and generalization may create the illusion that work is being done by the patient. However, in retrospect, in the supervisory review, it is realized that very little of substance has been accomplished. Since time is of the essence, it is critical that nonproductive verbalizations must be converted to become productive, either by interpretation of the vagueness and generalization as serving a defensive function, or by confronting it in a manner that blocks the patient from continuing in this mode, thus elevating his anxiety level and evoking an effective response, as Davanloo does, or by systematic inquiry as to specific details that the patient is avoiding by vagueness or generalization.

In Chapter 6 we see how Dr. Been does the latter on several occasions. For instance, when the patient tells him, "I have many women friends," he asks for a specific example. She responds with a name, but is again vague and general about their interaction. When Dr. Been again makes inquiry as to the specifics of their interaction, asking "What do you talk about?" the barriers to closeness become revealed. Without inquiry, one might get the general impression that she has many satisfactory relationships with women, which is not the case.

Later, Dr. Been describes the importance of having the patient distinguish between his parents, keeping clear those feelings having to do with mother and those having to do with father. So long as the patient lumps them together and talks about his or her "parents" in a global fashion, the conflicts relating to the oedipal focus will not emerge.

Immediacy

Attendance to what is going on in the transference allows for the connection of thought, feeling, and impulse at the experiential level. The therapist should be alert to nonverbal signs that the patient is experiencing something he is not reporting. This should be attended to with such inquiry as, "What are you experiencing?" or "What's going on?"

Interpreting Upward

Inasmuch as there are bound to be perseverating preoedipal issues with every oedipal patient — unresolved orality in psychosexual terms, rapprochement issues in object relations terms, or narcissistic vulnerability in self-psychology terms — one has to make a clinical decision when these issues emerge. They can be interpreted with the earlier developmental metapsychology as an organizing principle, but if we do this we encourage or facilitate a more regressive stance vis-a-vis the treatment process and transferentially. Since regression is to be avoided in brief therapy, we interpret this same material within the context of the oedipal triangle and its conflicts. The fear of maternal punishment by the withholding of maternal support or love is interpreted as a consequence of the competitive strivings vis-a-vis the father. The narcissistic wound of the oedipal defeat is interpreted within the framework of the competitive evaluation of the self vis-a-vis the rival. If the patient is unable to work with this kind of material within the oedipal framework, but seems traumatized by such interpretations, we have to assume that he is not a candidate for this approach.

Maintaining the Focus

The definition of a therapeutic focus at the start of brief treatment is part of the evaluation process, i.e., the determination whether or not it is possible to define the problem in terms of a specific conflict that can be uncovered and worked through in a relatively brief time period. As Dr. Been notes, the recognition of more complicated psychological situations may indicate that the individual is not suitable for this approach. The interpretation upward is an example of how the focus on the oedipal conflict is maintained even in the presence of issues that can be otherwise conceptualized. If the problem is not focal, the patient is not a candidate for brief treatment. Assuming that the selection is appropriate, all material introduced by the patient should be conceptualized within the framework of the Oedipus complex, if this is the theoretical organizing principle being used to start with. Other forms of brief treatment (Mann 1973, Malan 1976) may formulate other focal conflicts as their organizing principle, e.g., issues such as loss. If the focus is not maintained, we may find ourselves on the road to a more traditional long-term treatment.

Monitoring and Interpretation of the Transference

Transference *reactions* to the therapist are reactions primarily based on past relationships rather than on the reality of who the therapist is, or on the reality of the nature of the therapeutic relationship.

These reactions are based on *current wishes and/or fears*, however, despite their origin in the past.

Transference resistance refers to a manner of relating to the therapist that is intended, consciously or unconsciously, to make certain infantile wishes come true and/or to prevent what is feared from coming about. This way of relating — *to bring about a pre-determined outcome in the relationship* — will also be characteristic of the individual's manner of relating in other relationships about which he is in conflict.

Transference reactions are more likely to be conscious and reported by the patient inasmuch as they are specific to the immediate situation and are experienced as such. The patient may say, "I feel like you are criticizing me." The transference resistances that are characterological are more likely to be unconscious and to be built into the manner of relating than into the material proper. These characterological defensive postures which are played out in the treatment relationship are more likely to slip by and even be colluded with by the therapist who is not vigilant for such an eventuality. In particular, defenses that would fall in the general category of passivity tend to elicit the inappropriate taking of responsibility by the therapist in a collusive resistance to the unconscious competitive strivings of the patient and to unconscious hostilities toward the therapist.

Giving advice or answering the patient's questions may stand in collusion with such avoidance as well as with infantile dependency wishes. Although these dependency wishes might be appropriately facilitated in long-term treatment aimed at analyzing them, such an approach is not suitable in brief treatment.

Interpreting the transference includes what the patient is doing and why he is doing it. The consistent elucidation of the dynamics prevents the establishmet of a hard-core transference neurosis.

Since every action of the therapist will inevitably have an associated reaction on the part of the patient, interpretation of the transference itself may elicit a transference reaction. For example, it may be experienced as criticism. This also needs to be attended to and explored.

The term "exploiting" the transference refers to the use of positive transferential feelings of the patient toward the therapist for the purpose of bringing about a therapeutic goal. Freud (1917,

p. 443) referred to the unobjectionable positive transference, and the establishment of a therapeutic alliance depends to some degree on these positive feelings, or to what Erikson (1950) might see as "basic trust." Freud notes that a transference is present in the patient from the start of therapy and that for a while it is the most powerful motive in the advance of the process. He adds that we need not bother about it as long as it operates in favor of the analytic work, but that we must turn our attention to it when it becomes a resistance (Freud 1917, p. 443). The greater the degree of distortion of reality contained in those positive feelings, and the more they stand in opposition to thoughts, feelings, or impulses that would endanger them, the more they become a resistance and must be interpreted. A basic trust that is consistent with the present reality, although it is derived from the past, is currently adaptive and even necessary to the alliance.

Any actions or statements by the patient that allude to the treatment situation should be explored by the therapist in a here and now interpersonal focus, relating it to the therapeutic focus that was determined at the start of treatment to be the core issue. Examples of situations where this has become evident are lateness, the patient talking in generalities about her reactions to authority figures, bringing up old therapists, complaining about doctors or about therapy in a general fashion.

In the course of the interpretation of transference, it should be noted if there is a passive compliance and agreement as contrasted to using the material actively in a working alliance.

The following are examples of transference-related material or behavior:

Wishes to please the therapist
   Overly compliant behavior
   Seductive behavior
   Ingratiating behavior
   Bringing gifts
   Taking care of the therapist
   Asking the therapist for advice
Avoidance of displeasing the therapist
   Avoidance of negative material (anger, envy, criticism, competitiveness

> Avoidance of sexual material or sexual feelings toward the therapist
>
> Avoidance of negative perceptions of the self, or overuse of negative statements about the self to induce therapist support.

Such transference reactions or postures may be subtle. When the patient compliments the therapist on an astute observation, one has to look at how the patient feels about the therapist for making it. Behind the compliment may well hide competitive envy or resentment.

USE OF COUNTERTRANSFERENCE REACTIONS

Countertransference reactions that are not specific to unresolved conflicts, and the defenses against them on the part of the therapist, provide a clue about what is going on in the transference. For example, passive-aggressive withholding behavior may evoke anger in the therapist. Feelings of sexual excitement in the therapist may be a response to the patient's covert seductiveness.

EXTRA-THERAPY CONTACTS

As in long-term treatment, if something unusual happens that involves both patient and therapist, and the patient does not bring it up, the therapist should, exploring the meaning of the event within the framework of the focus. For example, meeting the patient in the elevator or in the bathroom (more anxiety provoking for both therapist and patient) will elicit fantasies and feelings that may lead to intensified resistance if they are ignored.

IMPASSE IN TREATMENT

We may say with some degree of certainty that when there is an impasse in treatment, long or brief, it is due to unanalyzed transference resistances that are being acted out in the treatment situation. We cannot afford to let such an impasse go on in brief therapy for obvious reasons. The therapist's resistance to exploring the patient's resistance should be attended to promptly in supervision. For the therapist in private practice who does not have supervisory oversight, energetic self-supervision is essential to the success of brief treatment.

THE TRIADS OF INTERPRETATION

The triad of conflict, anxiety, and defense is explored within the determined focus. For example, the anxiety and guilt associated with the conflict between the wish to love and the wish to compete with the parent of the same sex is defended against with a reaction formation in which aggression is transformed to placating behavior and turned against the self.

The oedipal focus is on the triangular interpersonal situation with mother, father, and patient. Both legs of the triangle must be explored and then interrelated with respect to parents as well as in the context of derivative triangles.

The focus is explored within the triad of past relationships, present day relationships, and the transference. For example, the wish to be special to father, the wish to be special with the boss, and the wish to be special with the therapist are tied together dynamically. The presence of the same conflict, anxiety, and defense in each of these situations is explored.

References

Erikson, E. (1950). *Childhood and Society*. New York: Norton.

Freud, S. (1912). The dynamics of transference. *Standard Edition* 12:99–108. London: Hogarth.

———. (1917). General theory of the neuroses: Transference. *Standard Edition* 16:431–447. London: Hogarth.

Malan, D. (1976). *The Frontier of Brief Psychotherapy*. New York: Plenum Press.

Mann, J. (1973). *Time-Limited Psychotherapy*. Cambridge: Harvard University Press.

Chapter 5·

AN EGO PSYCHOLOGICAL APPROACH
TO EVALUATION

ALTHEA J. HORNER, PH.D.

The first step toward successful brief psychotherapy is the selection of candidates who are suitable for this approach. As Dr. Been notes in Chapter 6, the major necessary ego capacities, in general, are:

1. The ability to form meaningful give-and-take relationships.
2. The ability to tolerate strong affects associated with anger, guilt, depression, and anxiety.
3. Characterological flexibility.
4. Positive response to interpretation.

Dr. Been reports the critical questions that Sifneos poses for evaluation of suitability for short-term anxiety-provoking psychotherapy (STAPP), on page 100.

As part of the research project, a rating scale for the assessment of ego functioning was developed (Horner and Pollack) and operationally defined for teaching purposes. Two items assessing superego functioning were included to determine the adequacy of guilt and shame modulation. The evaluation interview(s) should provide the data on which these conclusions may be drawn. The following items to be evaluated are also presented in the form of the original chart (see Appendix).

Ego and Superego Functions Operationally Defined

EGO FUNCTIONS

Relation to Reality

1. Good reality testing
   Patient can distinguish between wishes/fears and reality.
2. Sense of self as real
   Allowing for defensive depersonalization, patient experiences himself as real most of the time.
3. Can look at self objectively
   Patient can stand back and ally himself with the interviewer to explore the patient's wishes, feelings, beliefs, and actions.

Regulation and Control of Instinctual Drives

1. Capacity for delay
   Patient adapts readily to the delays of the intake process and can tolerate frustration of wishes.
2. Adequate impulse control
   Patient can talk about sexual or aggressive impulses without having to discharge them into action.
3. Capacity for adaptive expression
   Control of sexual and aggressive impulses is not too rigid to allow for their appropriate expression in reality.

Object relations

1. Basic trust
   Patient sees at least one person as benign and trustworthy.
2. Relatedness
   Patient is emotionally present and interpersonally engaged during the interview.
3. Differentiation
   Patient is able to perceive the interviewer and others as separate and different from himself.
4. Stability
   Patient can work with transference interpretations without losing a realistic perception of the interviewer.

5. Integration
   Patient can tolerate ambivalence toward himself and others.
6. Maturity
   Patient has been able to establish and maintain true peer relationships.
   Patient has history of altruistic relationships.

Thought Processes

Patient can think conceptually and logically.

Defenses

1. Adequacy
   Patient can tolerate negative and positive affect (anxiety, depression, guilt, shame, anger, love, affection, pleasure).
   Patient can talk about negative and positive affects.
   Patient can recover readily from a regressive reaction and talk about it.
2. Flexibility
   Flexibility of defenses allows for their examination in the interview.
3. Maturity
   Major defenses used are the more advanced ones of intellectualization, sublimation, repression, rationalization, or displacement without significant recourse to more primitive modes of projection, externalization, somatization, denial, or introjection.

Autonomous Functions

1. Relative independence from conflict
   Speech, cognition, perception, or motor behavior are not impaired in life or in the interview because of psychological reasons.
2. Recoverability
   If these functions are partially impaired, this can be understood and worked with in a psychological context by the patient.
3. Organic integrity
   There are no neurological disorders that would cause impairment that interfered with the ability to do the work of the interview.

Synthetic Functions

1. Psychological mindedness
   Patient is able to think in terms of psychological cause and effect.
2. Capacity for insight
   Patient is able to draw valid psychological conclusions with respect to his own feelings, wishes, thoughts, and behavior.

SUPEREGO FUNCTIONS

Conscience

1. Standards of right and wrong
   Patient wants to live according to established standards of right and wrong.
2. Capacity for guilt
   Patient experiences guilt when he fails to meet these standards.
3. Realistic
   Standards do not require unrealistic perfection of morality.

Ego-Ideal

1. Feelings of worth
   Patient has well-established sense of himself as a worthwhile person.
2. Realistic
   Patient's image of himself does not require unrealistic perfection or reveal grandiosity.

Clinical and Research Usefulness

In the BAP training seminar it was found that where there was wide divergence of ratings by participants, problems often arose in therapy that suggested the unsuitability of the patient for the brief approach.

The rating scale (Appendix) is included in this book to enhance the proper selection of candidates for this technique, either in the private consultation room, or for research purposes.

Reference

Horner, A. and Pollack, J. (in preparation). *Brief Adaptation-Oriented Psychotherapy: Manual.* New York: Beth Israel Medical Center Department of Psychiatry.

Chapter 6

THE CLINICAL INTERVIEW: ASSESSMENT AND DEFINITION OF THE FOCUS

HAROLD BEEN, M.D.

In this chapter the process of selecting patients appropriate for short-term psychotherapy involving a simple oedipal focus is discussed and illustrated. The patients who are appropriate for this form of short-term treatment present with neurotic symptoms: anxiety, inhibitions, phobias, problems in achievement in school or work, and/or interpersonal difficulties. The goals of the evaluation are both to understand the psychodynamic and genetic basis of the patient's problems and to determine if these problems will be amenable to the techniques of short-term psychotherapy. Therefore, the evaluation serves as both a diagnostic tool and a trial of the effectiveness of the technique for the particular patient.

In the past two decades there has been an extensive study and development of techniques of short-term dynamic psychotherapy, particularly by Sifneos (1972, 1979), Malan (1963, 1976), and Davanloo (1978, 1980). They have each separately developed techniques that are designed to uncover and work through specific types of conflicts in a psychoanalytic framework in a relatively short period of time. The evaluation process is heavily influenced by the nature of the conflicts to be worked through, the desired end result, and the personal style of the evaluator.

In this book the predominant focus is the short-term psychotherapy of relatively uncomplicated oedipal problems. Therefore, the evaluation process of patients with these problems is discussed in greater detail. However, it is also important to keep in mind the recognition of more complicated psychological situations in order to assess the need for changes in technique appropriate to these clinical situations. References to these techniques are also included.

Comparison with Classical Technique

The evaluation process for short-term dynamic psychotherapy differs from the process for more classical psychoanalytic treatments, paralleling the differences in therapeutic strategy. In classical technique, therapeutic regression to promote the development of a complete transference neurosis is the desired means of achieving a therapeutic cure. The technique relies on free association. Conversely, in short-term psychotherapy the resolution of neurotic conflict is achieved by the avoidance of therapeutic regression and of the subsequent development of a transference neurosis. The technique requires active maintenance of the dynamic focus and constant transference interpretation on the part of the therapist. This approach creates a different therapeutic atmosphere that requires the patient to possess specific ego capacities.

Patients with a relatively simple, focused conflict related to oedipal material can be interviewed without much attention paid to characterological issues; the interview has a cognitive flavor. Patients on the other end of the neurotic spectrum, with many characterological problems such as obsessional defenses, passivity, and dependency, require much more immediate attention to characterological resistance in order to assess the patient's potential for effective responsiveness. These interviews, using techniques developed by Davanloo (1978, 1980), have a flavor that is less cognitive and more confrontive. In this book, greater attention is paid to the simpler patients, thus the Sifneos (1979) technique is more extensively illustrated.

Assessing Ego Assets of
Patients for Short-Term Psychotherapy

In their work with short-term psychotherapy, Malan (1963, 1976) Sifneos (1972, 1979) and Davanloo (1978, 1980) all agree that there are certain ego capacities that are necessary for patients to succeed in this form of intensive treatment. It is critical in the evaluation process to establish the presence of these assets. The following are the major necessary ego capacities:

1. The ability to form meaningful give-and-take relationships
2. The ability to tolerate strong affects associated with anger, guilt, depression, and anxiety
3. Characterological flexibility
4. Positive response to interpretation

Assessing the Quality of Interpersonal Relationships

All of the above ego assets are evaluated within their interpersonal context. The ability to form meaningful give-and-take relationships is a prime indication of a patient's psychological development beyond early narcissistic object relationships. This capacity informs the evaluator that the patient has a sufficient degree of characterological maturity to withstand the anxiety generated in short-term treatment without the danger of severe characterological regression. This aspect of a patient's personality is evaluated by exploring the patient's relationships in childhood, adolescence, and adulthood. Frequently this information is difficult to evaluate, particularly in the relationships of early childhood. The ability of a patient to make an important sacrifice, in moderation, in consideration of another person's needs, is prime evidence in this regard. However, when trying to elicit this material in early childhood, the normal, self-centered, dependent behaviors of early childhood make differentiation between the normal narcissism of childhood and pathological narcissism very difficult. For example, a 40-year-old woman reports that she had a wonderful relationship with her mother in early years in which she received much "love and affection." When looking at this relationship more closely, the patient states that she received many material things and frequent physical demonstrations of affection. She also speaks of frequently making sacrifices for her mother in order to please her, such as cleaning up her room, washing the dishes, and trying to be helpful when her mother was ill. All of this is reported with appropriate affect, and on the surface the relationship appears to be one of give and take. However, this information in isolation does not really allow us to distinguish if this patient is relating to her mother in a genuinely altruistic manner or is relating in a defensive, compliant manner based on strictly narcissistic or dependent yearnings. It becomes easier to evaluate these relationships in adolescence and adulthood, when one can frequently explore with greater clarity the presence or absence of meaningful give-and-take relationships with peers as opposed to parental authority figures. In these relationships the capacity to give to another important person with occasional self-sacrifice without a compliant or masochistic pattern can more easily be determined. The chumships in latency, the adolescent friendships with both sexes, and the more intimate enduring adult sexual relationships are explored to assess the absence of exploitive, power-oriented, self-aggrandizing behaviors characteristic of borderline, narcissistic individuals. One also looks for evidence of underlying schizoidal detachment. For example, the same 40-year-old woman later describes her relationships with men as being totally characterized by a lack of spontaneity and a need to belittle and control. Although these behaviors are characteristic of nonaltruistic object relationships, they may be defensive in nature and based on oedipal pathology. When further exploring her relationships with women, this same patient claims to have many close female friends.

P: I have many women friends. We do things together all the time.

T: Tell me of one friend with whom you feel very close.

P: That is difficult. Let me see. (*Pause.*) Well, Martha and I see each other a few times a month for theater or concerts.

T: What do you talk about?

P: Well, you see, I don't really tell my friends my private affairs. I would not want to burden them. And I really want to have a good time. None of my women friends know that I have difficulties with men, or difficulties in my business. They think I'm really together.

T: So you don't really get close to women or men.

P: I never have let myself get close to anyone, really. (*Pause.*) I prefer my privacy.

Here again, the patient informs the evaluator of a real lack of capacity to form any intimate relationship in her current life. There is little likelihood of this patient's being able to tolerate an intimate exposure in intensive brief psychotherapy, particularly one focusing on an uncomplicated oedipal conflict.

The patient's object relations maturity can be gauged most accurately by the quality of the relationship with the therapist. Patients who interact responsively with a wide range of affect and a quality of thoughtful listening and responding possess qualities indicative of the presence of give-and-take relationships in their lives, even if historical information about these relationships is sparse. These qualities are revealed by the affective spontaneity and the flexibility of defenses used by the patient in the interview. Patients who are able to tolerate feelings of anger, guilt, and depressive longing and use a multitude of defenses reveal a maturity of character structure.

Characterological flexibility and affective responsiveness are frequently revealed to the therapist following an interpretation. For example, a 48-year-old woman who was experiencing marital difficulties initially denied having a good relationship with her father.

P: I never had much to do with my father. He was never home.

T: What do you remember about him?

P: (*Responds emotionally*) As I said, he was never home, so I really didn't know about him.

T: You knew nothing about his life?

P: (*Appears thoughtful*) I heard stories that he was a very charming, debonair man before he was married. (*Patient smiles*)

T: Are you aware you're smiling?

P: (*Blushing*) I remember once thinking that he must have lived his life in the university just like "The Student Prince."

T: So your father had been in your mind and you had exciting fantasies about him.

P: (*Thoughtfully*) It was really terrible how little I saw of him. I wanted so much to spend time with him. (*Pa-

tient has tears in her eyes.) I used to wait up at night hoping he would come home before I fell asleep.

T: How did you feel at that time?

P: Very sad. You know, you are making me feel very uncomfortable thinking about this.

The above interchange reveals a patient who, after an initial denial, is able to respond with increasing affective depth and flexibility as her relationship with her father is explored. The patient also begins to experience an increasing intensity in relation to the therapist. This patient clearly has the ability to listen, respond, and relate affectively to the therapist with a positive response to interpretation. With interchanges of this quality occurring during the interview, the evaluator can be certain that this patient has the capacity for give-and-take relationships without obtaining memories of such relationships in early childhood or even in adolescence. The patient also demonstrates relative characterological flexibility, making focus on a simple oedipal conflict possible.

The above patient's response to interpretation is a highly significant predictor of successful brief psychotherapy. This patient is able to engage with increasing depth of affect along with cognitive awareness as the evaluator continues to focus on her relationship with her father. After the patient relates her discomfort the interview continues.

T: Can you describe your sadness?

P: (*Hesitatingly*) I feel near tears, you know. I can't believe this. But I really feel how much I missed him. It's really very sad. (*Patient sobs.*)

T: So you can accept that you have needed to keep your feelings about your father buried in order not to feel this pain.

P: (*Thoughtfully*) I think you're right. Do you think this has something to do with my problems with my husband that we discussed earlier?

Here one sees that this patient continues to respond to the therapist's statements with a deepening awareness of her feelings and an awakening parallel cognitive thrust toward exploring her problems.

Such responses are further indicative of this patient's capacity for give-and-take in a relationship and also reveal heightened motivation to continue the therapeutic exploration. Had the patient denied the consequences of her feelings and showed very little interest in the material, one would seriously question her ability to work in this form of treatment.

As seen above, the four major assets of (1) ability to form a meaningful give-and-take relationship, (2) ability to tolerate strong affects, (3) characterological flexibility, and (4) a positive response to interpretation are all factors that provide clues to the potential success of brief intensive psychotherapy. All four of these assets are also different manifestations of a patient's core relatedness and reflect maturity of object relationships. They are not necessarily informative about the underlying psychodynamics, but they do reveal a characterological integration of sufficient strength and resilience to tolerate an intensive, aggressive psychotherapeutic approach.

Besides the above four issues, Sifneos (1972, 1979), Malan (1963, 1976), and Davanloo (1978, 1980) have discussed the importance of motivation and psychological-mindedness in evaluating the potential success of patients in brief intensive psychotherapy. It is well known that patients who are better motivated to make changes will do better in any psychotherapy. Patients who recognize that their problems are psychological and are not looking for magical solutions to these problems present the therapist of any persuasion with a less difficult situation. However, very often the only true evaluation of motivation for treatment occurs during the course of the evaluation when one can assess if a patient is involved in the exploration of his problems as resistances are challenged and current figure-past figure linkages are explored. Patients who might have been poorly motivated initially, as measured by their knowledge of their symptoms or by their initial expectations, may show changes that indicate a shift in their outlook toward receiving treatment during the course of the evaluation. In summary, motivation for treatment is best evaluated in the course of the developing interaction with the therapist.

There are other concrete issues mentioned in Sifneos' (1972, 1979) criteria for evaluating patients for short-term anxiety-provoking psychotherapy (STAPP) that can be helpful in assessing motivation. These are listed below in the form of questions.

1. Can the patient recognize that the symptoms are psychological in origin?
2. Is the patient honest in reporting about himself?
3. Is the patient willing to participate actively in the evaluation?
4. Is the patient introspective and actively curious about himself?
5. Does the patient really desire to change and not simply to have the symptoms removed?
6. Are the expectations for the results of the treatment realistic (i.e., not grandiose, magical, etcetera)?
7. Is the patient willing to make a reasonable and tangible sacrifice (e.g., see the therapist at a mutually convenient time, pay a reasonable fee, etcetera)?
8. Does the patient give evidence now and/or in the past of an ability to change and try new behaviors?
9. Is the patient very distressed by the behaviors or problems he hopes to change?

The issue of psychological-mindedness or intelligence is very difficult to evaluate. Clearly it is the responsiveness to the interview that is crucial. Obviously, a bright patient with the capacity to introspect can move more quickly in treatment than a more concrete individual. However, these intellectual capacities are often used in the service of defense, whereas an initially concrete person is often stimulated by the evaluation to become more introspective.

Exploring the Psychodynamics and Structure

Exploration of the psychodynamic conflicts and characterological structure is a critical part of the evaluation. Although this exploration can not be separated procedurally from the exploration and assessment of the ego assets, it is necessary to do so for the purpose of discussion.

As in most psychiatric interviews, the initial part of the evaluation consists of clarifying the presenting psychiatric history and the present psychosocial context of the symptomatology. An attempt is made to clarify quickly if there are any psychiatric characterological conditions that would preclude short-term intensive psychotherapy. The following are negative criteria: (1) psychotic or borderline character structure; (2) presence of acute biological illness, unipolar or bipolar illness; (3) history of grossly destructive or self-destructive behavior now or in the past, including suicide attempts; (4) severe impulse disorders; (5) history of drug addiction or alcohol abuse in the present or past five years; and (6) history of psychiatric hospitalization. If any of the above criteria are met, the patient should be referred for other forms of treatment.

The next issues to be evaluated are the characterological defenses. If the defensive style is very rigid and inflexible as described under "Evaluation of Ego Assets," the patient will present greater difficulties for brief intensive psychotherapy. Obsessional defenses with characterological passivity and dependence need to be challenged quickly in the evaluation according to the techniques devised by Davanloo (1978, 1980). These defenses usually indicate a more severe degree of character pathology than is shown by the patients discussed in this book. However, if a highly challenging, confrontative technique is used, a patient with long-standing characterological pathology can also be treated in short-term intensive psychotherapy with the exploration of multiple foci.

Assuming the patient under evaluation has adequate ego assets, relatively mild character pathology, and no psychiatric contraindications, one can assume that the individual is relatively healthy and intact. The therapist then proceeds to evaluate the underlying oedipal focus which explains the symptoms in their present psychosocial context. Here one follows a procedure similar to that designed by Sifneos (1979) for STAPP patients.

The major task is to find evidence in childhood, adolescence, and adulthood of the unfolding oedipal triangular conflicts that remain unresolved. To do this the evaluator first has to help the patient to reformulate his or her present difficulties in interpersonal terms. For example, a male patient may initially present with stated "work problems." After discussing these difficulties of poor work performance, difficulty in concentration and anxiety while working, the patient discusses his anxiety-laden relationship with his new female boss. The patient then begins to realize that his current work difficulties began when this new boss replaced his former male boss. The patient had not previously made this connection and is now able to see his problem in the interpersonal framework uncovered in the interview. The establishment of the interpersonal framework of the present conflict is absolutely necessary if one is going to further attempt to uncover the genetic oedipal focus which was originally interpersonal in nature.

Often the patient has many problems. The evaluator then wants to test the patient's ability to select one focus of an interpersonal nature on which to work exclusively in the therapy. For example, a 29-year-old male graduate student expresses dissatisfaction with his studies, career goal confusion, and difficulties with his current girlfriend. To work in brief intensive psychotherapy with an uncomplicated oedipal focus, the patient will have to accept confining the therapy to the interpersonal problems with his girlfriend. It is often true that in the healthier patients, the other problems may be intimately connected to the main therapeutic focus. They may also be alleviated with successful working through of the focus. However, in the case of the student just described, no active attempt is made to focus on career or school problems. In less healthy patients, whose characterological issues are also paramount, the short-term psychotherapy is geared toward dealing with multifocal problems underlying the major characterological pathology. If the above patient presented with obsessional defenses, passivity, and dependency as part of characterological pathology, all the patient's area of disturbance would need to be explored using Davanloo's (1978, 1980) methods. An uncomplicated oedipal focus could not be isolated for resolution.

Once the patient has accepted a single focus in his current life and this current focus has been fully explored in an interpersonal framework, the genetic focus is explored.

The genetic focus for healthier patients is usually the oedipal focus, with the assumption that any pregenital issues are defensive regressions. The other assumptions made when dealing with these healthier patients are that whatever unresolved mourning is present can be totally handled within the oedipal triangular situation and that the relationship with both oedipal parents was primarily positive, even though ambivalent. When highly ambivalent relationships were present with either parent, with very strong unconscious negative feelings, it is likely that there will be significant character pathology, often of an obsessional nature with problems of passivity, dependency, and more severe anxiety. These problems can be further compounded by the actual death of the parents or by the development or displacement of these triangular conflicts onto the wider family, i.e., siblings, aunts, uncles, grandparents, etcetera. These difficulties complicate the treatment and would prevent an exclusive focus on the simple oedipal issue.

By the time the current problems are clear and placed into an interpersonal context, the evaluator will have made an assessment of the ego assets of the patient and the appropriateness of the patient for short-term intensive psychotherapy. The remaining problem facing the evaluator is to help the patient find the genetic focus and tie it together with the current delineated interpersonal problem. The best approach in uncovering the genetic focus is to take a systematic history of the patient from early childhood through adolescence and into adulthood.*

The technique of inquiry involves using a combination of leading questions to check facts and to stimulate unconscious processes. When first observing an evaluation of this type, a more traditional psychotherapist will often feel that the patient is being led or that thoughts are being "placed in" the patient's head. Actually, the leading questions are meant to test the patient's emotional responses and resistances to working with repressed oedipal material. As the interview proceeds, the evaluator can judge whether the patient's responses are in the nature of compliance to the evaluator or represent a genuine interchange. For example, a 30-year-old man has problems competing with his male peers in business. During the evaluation, the patient reveals that he becomes passive with his colleagues, often at times when more appropriate competitive, assertive behavior is indicated. When discussing his early history, he reveals that he had a warm, close relationship with his mother until aged 4, at which time a younger brother, Tim, was born. He would spend considerable time sitting in a hallway playing with his toys, while his mother was holding and feeding his younger brother.

т: So you sat outside the room, unnoticed and quiet.

---

*Editor's note: The capacity to delay and to forego gratification is demonstrated by the patient's cooperativeness in the history-taking process. If compliance is a significant aspect of this cooperation, it will be evident in other interactions as well and thus interpretable.

P: Yes. My mother was so busy and happy taking care of Tim.

T: But what happened to your close relationship with her?

P: I don't know. I never thought about that.

T: How did you feel toward Tim?

P: I liked him very much. He was so cute, and we are so close now.

T: So Tim arrived and occupied center stage with your mother.

P: That's true. But I accepted it. Occasionally I got jealous of him when he played with my toys. Once I hit him hard on the head when he played with one of my toy soldiers.

T: So, it's clear you felt very angry when Tim played with something you wanted. Certainly not a passive response.

P: Yes, that's true. But aren't all kids that way?

T: So when Tim went into your mother's lap, that place you liked so much, you sat passively in the hall. I wonder how you felt.

P: I think you are stretching it.

T: So, how did you behave with your colleague John last weekend at the board meeting?

P: Well, I told you already I was passive! But I was burning inside. John knew that the boss was giving him points so he continued to show off.

T: So with John you were passive outside, but burning inside. Can't we say that you handled Tim's birth also by becoming passive outside and burning inside?

Later in the interview the patient reveals that both he and Tim were swimmers in their high school. The patient's mother would rarely attend his swim meets, but she rarely missed an event in which Tim was competing. The patient again confirms that he resented Tim's relationship with his mother during his adolescence but again remained entirely passive in expressing his feelings. This pattern was again connected to current relationships with colleagues.

All questions asked while taking the genetic history are focused. The evaluator can choose to concentrate on those areas that offer the greatest rewards, e.g., evaluating in detail the relationship with a male sibling, as above, when a patient has competitive problems with men. Other aspects of the development picture, such as career choice, etcetera, need not be as detailed.

Oedipal Period—Childhood

To develop the early oedipal period, the following questions are useful. The therapist asks initially for the earliest memory. These screen memories often reveal significant dynamic constellations and issues crucial to understanding the inner life of the patient.

For example, one male patient whose chief problems centered around difficulties with females reported the following early memory at aged 3 to 4: "I was walking with my mother who was taking my older sister to kindergarten. My sister went through the black gate, into school. We were never as close again. I was very sad." The patient's genetic problem centered around early sexual feelings toward both mother and sister and his resultant anger stemming from being "cut off" from both of them. The screen memory is often a clear signpost to the core genetic conflicts.

Specific questions about the patient's relationship to each parent should be asked. When patients answer questions about either parent with global statements about both parents or family members, the patient is asked to be specific about a particular parent. For example, a 24-year-old male responds to the therapist's question about the nature of his mother's physical handling of him when he was a child by saying the following:

> P: Dad and Mom were very affectionate with me and would put me on their laps when they would tell me stories.
>
> T: But how did your mother treat you?
>
> P: Well, Mom was like I said before. She would put me on her lap like Dad.

T: But was there any difference between when your father did this and when your mother did?

P: (*Hesitating*) Well, you know, when Mother did this she would hug me and give me a kiss, and she smelled so good. She was always soft and warm and had this warm laugh.

It is important with the above patient to have him be very specific and distinguish between his parents. When patients can't distinguish clearly their feelings and memories for a specific parent, the chances of developing a meaningful oedipal focus is very poor.[†]

When evaluating the early memories of the patient's relationship with his parents, the question of which parent the patient felt closer to is very important, along with the patient's perception of his or her ranking among the siblings with either parent. Frequently, patients will have memories of nightmares at aged 5 or 6, or other behavior that brought the patient to the parents' bed. Here the manner in which the patient handled these episodes is very informative. For example, the 48-year-old woman with marital difficulty, discussed earlier, denies any meaningful relationship with her father. The patient reveals that at aged 5 or 6 she often went to her parents' bedroom at night and lay in the crack between her parents' beds, which were pushed together. She was afraid to move toward her father's side. At this point the patient reiterates her belief that there was no meaningful relationship between her and her father. This again leads to a discussion of what she knows of her father before his marriage. The patient then repeats that she often heard relatives discussing her father's cheerful life as a university student.

P: Yes, he was supposedly a wonderful dancer, singer and bon vivant.

T: He sounds very romantic.

[†]*Editor's note*: The oedipal level of development is characterized by the three-way relationship in which both objects are highly and uniquely valued and related to differentially. It is because *both* are important to the child that conflict develops. The preoedipal level is characterized by dyadic relationships in which the third party is an interloper or a spoiler and is not valued per se. The presence of the two parallel objects tells us the patient has developed to the oedipal level and is potentially suitable for the brief approach.

P: (*Blushing*) You know, that's true. I never put it that way, but I remember trying to think about him as a romantic younger man.

T: Do you realize you're blushing?

P: (*Anxiously moving about*) Well, maybe I had some feelings toward my father. (*In a joking fashion*) You don't suppose I felt that way when I was lying in the crack of the bed. (*Anxious laughter*)

It is important to note that in the above patient, defenses against conflictual material reappear during the interview and need to be reworked. This is to be expected and is consistent with standard psychoanalytic procedure.

This vignette illustrates how a patient can be brought to explore repressed relationships with parents by asking pertinent questions aimed at stimulating unconscious oedipal material. In this form of therapy the questions are often chosen for the purpose of stimulating such material.

During the early period, the patient's relationships with siblings, grandparents, aunts, uncles, maids, etcetera, are explored to find how the oedipal conflicts may have been displaced onto other important people and how siblings distort the oedipal development. These issues are exceedingly important. Some patients need to work through oedipal material with grandparents, aunts, uncles, etcetera, before they can deal with the triangular relationship with their parents. In the evaluation an overall idea of the complexity of these arrangements must be assessed to gauge the course of the therapy and its possible duration. For example, a 26-year-old male with recurrent difficulties remaining in relationships with women reports that as a child he lived a block from his grandparents' home. In evaluating his oedipal relationships, it becomes clear that the patient had an intense relationship with his maternal grandmother. He was her favorite grandchild. His grandfather frequently became irritated at his extensive visits and would become overtly angry at times with the patient, telling him to go home. The patient reports this with much feeling, whereas the struggle with his own parents is much more deeply repressed. The material related to the grandparents would be worked through initially during treatment. The material related to the parents would emerge later.

The birth of siblings and the effect on the patient's relationships with his parents are often quite traumatic. Should these births occur during the oedipal period, an understanding of their effect on the patient is essential. The new siblings may actually triumph over the patient in relation to the desired parent, stimulating feelings of loss of the oedipal love object along with feelings of rivalry.

Latency

The latency period should be explored to gather information about the type of resolution of the childhood oedipal conflicts. The relationship with peers, teachers and other authority figures outside the home are explored to gain further understanding of the patient's ego assets and developmental thrust.

Adolescence

Questions aimed at detailing the course of psychosexual maturation are asked. The patient's history of masturbation, dating patterns, and sexual relationships is elicited. The evaluator tries to determine how the patient's inner sexual life developed by asking the following types of questions, which are factual, while stimulating unconscious material.

1. When did your first learn about sex? Who told you?
2. How did this information affect your view of your parents?
3. Did you ever think of their sexual life?
4. Did you see either of your parents nude?
5. Did you know anything about your parents' sexual life?
6. When did you begin to masturbate? How did this affect your relationship with your parents?
7. How did you compare yourself physically to the parent of the same sex?
8. How did the opposite-sex parent feel about your developing body?
9. What did your first girlfriend/boyfriend look like? How did she/he compare to your opposite-sex parent?

10. When did you first have sexual relations, including intercourse?

The nature of friendships, relationships to authority, and school performance are again elicited to evaluate ego assets and the further developmental thrust.

Youth and Adulthood

Inquiries are directed toward understanding the major sexual relationships and the quality of the patient's separation from his original home. Career development is also briefly looked at. If the patient is married, detailed knowledge of the marital relationship, including the sexual relationship with the spouse and the relationship with children, if any, is sought. The relationships with spouses and/or lovers are very important, as they convey insights into the new rendition of the older oedipal struggles. Frequently a parent's relationship with his or her children may be a replay of a sibling relationship or a relationship with a parent.

After the history is taken, it should be possible to reconstruct the genetic basis for the current interpersonal difficulty. The oedipal focus may range from a simple lingering in the oedipal situation, with basically good early relationships with both parents on one side of the spectrum, to a midspectrum of a more complex oedipal situation in which grandparents, aunts, uncles, siblings, etcetera, are critical foci within the more general oedipal focus. As one then moves to more difficult patients, the oedipal focus is complicated by the loss focus, as discussed below.

Even with a complex oedipal focus, the patient may be suitable for a short-term anxiety-provoking psychotherapy modeled after the Sifneos approach if there are no complicating characterological problems or other foci resulting from the loss focus.

The Loss Focus

The loss focus centers around the experience of the loss of an important oedipal figure (e.g., a parent or sibling). The loss can be an actual one, such as the early loss of a parent through death, divorce, or other separation. The resulting grief will often be buried, producing chronic disturbances in psychosexual adaptation and resultant character pathology.

The loss can also be more of an internal, psychic phenomenon that results from severe ambivalence experienced toward a frustrating or rejecting oedipal figure. The intensity of this problem is even more complicated if the rejecting oedipal figure is of the opposite sex. The underlying murderous impulses can be deeply repressed, with resultant guilt, masochistic trends, and other character pathology, such as obsessional traits.

The degree of aggressive strivings, guilt, and depressive longings interwoven with ordinary oedipal strivings determines the complexity and depth of character pathology. In patients with a moderate to severe loss focus the modality of treatment required will be along the line of the approach developed by Malan (1963, 1976) and Davanloo (1978, 1980). In patients with a predominant oedipal focus, limited character pathology, and a mild degree of loss, a Sifneos (1972, 1979) model of therapy may be used. Frequently during the evaluation interview of an otherwise appropriate patient, it becomes imperative to determine if a loss focus is significantly complicating the oedipal focus. The following clinical example demonstrates this issue.

A 28-year-old single man with difficulties in his heterosexual relationship is speaking of his ambivalent relationship with his mother, when tears develop.

P: (*With tears in his eyes*) I really hated her when she used to speak to me like that. I could tell by the tone of her voice that I was being . . . dismissed!

T: Now you are weeping when you discuss this painful relationship with your mother. It is very important that we understand this.

P: (*Crying softly*) She was sure a bitch at times! But, you know, I still loved her. Sometimes she came through for me.

T: You continue to weep and it is obvious that you have strong mixed feelings about your relationship with your mother. But let's take a look. While you are weeping

> at this time, do you think you are crying more because you miss having the relationship you needed or because you have a lot of anger toward your mother for treating you on occasion in such a frustrating way?

P: (*Still crying, pauses*) That's a very difficult question. I don't know.

T: It's very important. Think about it.

P: I feel sad sometimes, but I really think I'm angry that she was sometimes less giving to me than I wished.

T: So you are saying that you were predominantly experiencing anger at your mother because she was not always as available to you as you wished.

P: Definitely

In this example the therapist is testing a patient without severe character pathology who starts to cry while talking about a primary oedipal figure who was not actually dead. It is critical to monitor the patient's response to assess the depth of the possible loss versus a less complicated positive oedipal position. Clearly in this case the patient indicates that he is predominantly experiencing the relationship with his mother in a relatively uncomplicated oedipal mode. Even though loss is in evidence, the tears are primarily a regressive mode of defense against the more negative feelings experienced in a basically positive relationship with his mother.

Had the above patient expressed feelings of greater deprivation and sadness, the therapist would have had to go into greater detail concerning the patient's dependent and passive longings. A brief therapy based on a simple oedipal focus would be unlikely to succeed.

Setting the Contract

As the interview moves toward closure, the evaluator has assessed in his own mind that the patient has the ego assets to withstand the anxiety of short-term psychotherapy. The patient has been able to select a single interpersonal focus that has a genetic link to a specific oedipal situation.

Once the genetic focus has been clarified and linked to the current complaint, a formulation is presented to the patient. For example, in the case of the 48-year-old married woman whose presenting problem focuses on her difficulties with her husband, the following formulation would be given to the patient by the therapist.

T: So we have seen that the difficulties in closeness with your husband parallel difficulties in closeness with your father. Clearly these patterns seem to be related, as we have repeatedly seen in our interview today.

The therapist then asks the patient if she will agree to work on this genetic focus in a brief treatment.

T: Do you think that if we focus on understanding your relationship with your father in a relatively short period of time this might help you with your current problems with your husband?

If the patient agrees to the contract, she is accepted into treatment.

Summary

The evaluation for short-term psychotherapy is both a diagnostic tool and a trial therapy. The successful evaluation ends with the therapist and patient agreeing to work on an oedipal genetic focus that is related to a clearly defined interpersonal problem. A carefully performed systematic evaluation is the most important basis for the selection of proper patients for short-term psychotherapy.

Only this procedure ensures a reasonable chance of a positive outcome and the avoidance of disappointment in both therapist and patient.

References

Davanloo, H. (1980). *Short-Term Dynamic Psychotherapy*. New York: Jason Aronson.

_____. (ed) (1978). *Basic Principles and Techniques in Short-Term*

Dynamic Psychotherapy. New York: SP Medical and Scientific Books.

Malan, D. (1963). *A Study of Brief Psychotherapy*. New York: Plenum Press.

_____. (1976). *The Frontier of Brief Psychotherapy*. New York: Plenum Press.

Sifneos, P. (1972). *Short-Term Psychotherapy and Emotional Crisis*. Cambridge: Harvard University Press.

_____. (1979). *Short-Term Dynamic Psychotherapy*. New York: Plenum Press.

Chapter 7

THE UNCOVERING PROCESS

ARNOLD WINSTON, M.D.
MANUEL TRUJILLO, M.D.

Steps of the Uncovering Process

According to the theoretical framework we are presenting, therapists attempting to help patients resolve oedipal conflicts must accomplish a specific set of goals (see Table 1, Chapter 2). Foremost among these is the uncovering of the basic oedipal wishes, i.e., the desire to defeat in competition and displace the same-sex parent in order to have a primary and erotic relationship with the parent of the opposite sex. The oedipal wishes, in turn, give rise to fears. There are fears related to the possible actualization of the wishes — the loss of control that might allow incest, patricide, or matricide. There are fears that the same-sex parent will detect the child's wishes and retaliate by withdrawing love or by further punishment in the form of castration or murder. On the other hand, the child may defeat the same-sex parent with resultant guilt and self-punishment. Family dynamics will greatly determine the intensity and specificity of each individual's fears. Thus, an overly permissive and/or overly sexualized family atmosphere may leave the oedipal child desperate for controls, whereas an atmosphere that is punitive, depriving, and depreciating will often escalate competition to murderous rage, with concomitant retaliatory fears. Lastly, one must also uncover the negative affects associated with the frustration of oedipal wishes, for example, the anger and disappointment of unrequited love, outrage and betrayal of partially requited love, the humiliation of defeat from a better-equipped rival, and the fear of being banished from the triangle for forbidden desires. Again, family dynamics, how and to what extent oedipal wishes are fostered and frustrated, and the child's basic endowment and development determine each patient's set of negative affects.

Each patient's particular constellation of wishes, fears, and negative affects is unique. Uncovering involves the systematic exploration of this constellation. Ideally, the patient comes to understand the origin of his or her constellation and comes to see how particular wishes, fears, and negative and positive affects now unconsciously govern major aspects of his life. The steps presented in Table 1 of Chapter 2 for uncovering are not necessarily sequential; rather they are an outline of what is to be consciously understood and experienced. A patient entering treatment has frequently repressed major aspects of his oedipal conflicts. He presents the therapist with derivatives of the oedipal conflict as well as with defenses against the conflict. The work of treatment begins with an agreement between patient and therapist to go beyond the defenses and the oedipal derivatives and to begin the uncovering of the core oedipal conflict.

Before discussing the technical aspects of uncovering it is useful to define the terms we are using and the theoretical approach on which this treatment is based. The short-term dynamic psychotherapy described here is based in large measure on analytic principles and on the major modifications proposed by Davanloo (1980) as well as Malan (1976a, b) and Sifneos (1979).

The Treatment Relationship

In short-term dynamic psychotherapy, as in classical analysis, there exist three simultaneous relationships between patient and therapist: the real relationship, the working alliance, and the transferential relationship.

In short-term dynamic psychotherapy, the real relationship is minimized as much as possible to prevent the gratification of instinctual or dependency wishes, in ways that prevent the analysis of these wishes, or in ways that prolong or subvert treatment. In practice the minimization of the real relationship is accomplished by maintaining a primarily analytic stance in relation to the patient. There should be careful adherence to time limits in sessions and to clear scheduling, billing, and payment regimens. Chatting with the patient on the way to the door or in the elevator carry with them the possibility of unknowingly gratifying the patient, inconsistently gratifying the patient, and possibly slighting the patient by inconsistent behavior. Although this does not doom therapy, it unnecessarily muddies the waters in a situation in which time is of the essence and in which real gratification and hurts must be carefully distinguished from transferential expectations and disappointments. In essence, the milieu of the working alliance extends portal to portal, the therapist maintaining the analytic stance throughout. In short-term dynamic psychotherapy the last thing one needs is "more grist for the mill."

The therapeutic alliance, as in classical treatment, is an artifact of the treatment situation involving a collaboration between the therapist's analytic stance and the observing ego of the patient. In brief therapy this alliance is the basic treatment matrix; without it treatment takes another form, e.g., supportive or directive. The therapist begins building this alliance from the first session onward and must keep sight of the alliance in each session. If transferential or other factors interfere with the therapeutic alliance, the therapist must intervene rapidly to prevent misalliance. This cannot be overstated, since oedipally focused work evokes powerful transferential feelings that can easily damage or break treatment, often with the unfortunate outcome of reconfirming the original oedipal trauma. For example, in the early work of one of our male therapists the working alliance with a young female patient had not been solidly built or attended to during treatment. As the patient began reexperiencing her sexual longings for a cold, rejecting father, both in treatment and in her current life, she experienced intense and bewildering pain. In a critical series of sessions the therapist explored and thus intensified her longings without simultaneously using the alliance to give her some perspective on her feelings. The patient terminated therapy humiliated and enraged, feeling once again that her sexuality and her attempt to be an adult woman led to misunderstanding and rejection from another important male (her therapist). Unspoken in the treatment was her transferential longing for the therapist and his countertransference avoidance of the subject. The working alliance most frequently breaks down when the transferential relationship is not properly managed.

We define the transferential relationship, following Greenson (1967), as those aspects of the relationship that are repetitive (from past important figures) and that involve needs and feelings that are irrational and inappropriate to the current situation. The analysis of these needs and feelings, particularly from the oedipal phase of development, is a critical component of this treatment. However, unlike classical treatment, regression is discouraged, and the transference neurosis is to be avoided.

Although the therapist is important, he is not to become the central figure in the patient's life. We attempt to avoid this in a number of ways. First, from the moment brief treatment starts, its ending is in sight. The patient, at least at a conscious level, knows that the therapist is available for a brief period of time and not until all is well or for any other indeterminate amount of time. The clarity of the ending allows the patient certain coping and distancing maneuvers that help prevent a dependent regression. The treatment is once weekly and is conducted face to face. Finally and most important, transference manifestations, particularly those that may lead to fantasized gratifications and dependency, are quickly interpreted to prevent fixed fantasies and unreal expectations. Lastly, patients chosen for this treatment have an object-relation capacity that does not necessitate the therapist becoming all-important, i.e., a transference neurosis.*

The Development and Agreement of a Focus

The last technical matter, which should be noted, refers to the scope of the work. In classical analysis a complete analysis is aimed at maximal growth, and all that is psychologically repressed falls within

---

Editor's note: The therapist's function as a "self-object" is not necessary for the maintenance of the cohesion or positive self-feeling of the patient (Stolorow and Lachmann (1980). A cohesive, evolved self with a modicum of self-esteem is already structured and available to the alliance in the properly selected patient.

the scope of treatment. The basic rule is free association. In short-term dynamic psychotherapy, the approach is focused. In the current treatment it is primarily an oedipal focus, and the basic rule is association within that focus.

One of the main factors in promoting uncovering in brief therapy is the systematic work done by both therapist and patient in establishing the therapeutic focus. This is discussed fully in Chapter 6, but a brief example will be presented here. A woman in her forties applied for treatment because she was not sure whether to stay in her marriage. She added that this was a particularly difficult decision for her because she had never loved any man and therefore could not really assess the situation with her husband. Her history revealed an early rejection by her mother and a strong, erotically tinged overevaluation of and overattachment to her father. Her face glowed when she talked of her father, and she stated with some pride that no man could measure up to her father in looks, humor, sophistication, intelligence, etcetera. The therapist repeatedly pointed out these manifestations of extreme attachment to her father. The therapist asked if her present need to have her father be the primary man in her life could be responsible for her stated inability to love a man and whether they should look at her marital problem in that light. The patient did see these connections and agreed to focal work involving an understanding of marital conflict based on an exploration of her early and current relationship to her parents.

The development and agreement of a focus are crucial in brief therapy. The agreement is one of a specific journey that allows both therapist and patient to know when the therapeutic work goes off course. Most importantly, the development of the focus mobilizes the patient, on both a conscious and an unconscious level, to seek relief in a particular exploration. It is typical for the evaluation session to begin the process of uncovering and the return of relevant repressed memories.

The other major facilitator for uncovering is the patient's inevitable reenactment of aspects of the oedipal dilemma with the therapist. With an opposite-sex therapist, longings for primary and erotic feelings are usually aroused, as well as the patient's characteristic defenses against the longings. With a same-sex therapist the competitive wishes and angry feelings and the defenses against these wishes and feelings usually predominate. At some level in each treatment the therapist is both mother and father. However, this may or may not be brought directly into treatment. In short-term dynamic psychotherapy transference interpretations are almost always made when the transference is used as a resistance. These transference interpretations often lead to new material, dreams, heightened affect, etcetera, and bring the experience into the consultation room.

In the first vignette the evaluation interview has already set the uncovering phase into motion, indicating that a therapeutic alliance has formed.

We will next present vignettes from three patients to illustrate the uncovering phase. Two of these cases will be continued into the chapters on "Working Through," "Resolution," and "Termination."

The first case is a relatively uncomplicated oedipal situation. The other cases present more complicated problems.

An Uncomplicated Oedipal Situation: Sandra G.

A married woman in her midthirties, Sandra G. has had panic attacks for the past three years. These attacks are well controlled by medications. The patient has requested treatment because she feels the anxiety is the symptom of an underlying problem that she wants to understand and deal with. She describes herself as happily married and able to function quite effectively as an administrator of afterschool programs for children. She has had three miscarriages and is upset and disappointed by her present inability to have a child. She had reconstructive surgery of the uterus after the first miscarriage, and she states that it is unclear if she will be able to carry a pregnancy to term. The anxiety began very suddenly three years ago when her husband asked her to take care of his mother, who was then bedridden and dying of cancer. During the evaluation interview she stated that she had always been strongly attached to her father — in fact she felt as if she was really his wife. She is the oldest of five children and she remembers running the home and caring for the children. She stated that her mother's only contribution was having the babies. She said that at adolescence her father pushed her away and she had been very hurt by this. She married in her early twenties and she reported several days of anxiety and depersonalization just prior to her marriage. Very early in her marriage she became pregnant and had an abortion because she was in school and felt unable to care for a child. She resents this bitterly and wonders if her miscarriages represent a punishment for her abortion. In talking about the onset of her anxiety she said that she had not wanted to disappoint her husband by refusing to care for his mother and felt guilty in not wanting to care for someone who was sick and dying. She also reported a prior anxiety attack that occurred after her first miscarriage. Her father visited her in the hospital and commented on her lipstick being smeared.

The therapist's hypothesis is that the patient's anxiety three years ago occurred because her husband's request that she care for his mother reactivated her oedipal conflicts. She did not want to share her husband with this incapacitated woman as she had shared her father with her mother, and on a deeper level the request had activated her unconscious death wishes toward her mother. The therapist feels that the patient's guilt over her abortion represents, in part, a displacement from death wishes toward her mother and guilt over her sexual wishes for her father. There is also unexpressed rage with both parents.

The patient was asked if her husband's request that she care for his mother had brought back conflicted feelings of caring for her siblings and the household. She said that the feelings were very similar and that she didn't want to let down either her father or her husband, and yet she felt neither one fully realized what he was asking of her. She added that she, too, did not really understand why her husband's request should trigger such emotions in her. She was asked if she wanted to explore her symptom as it related to her earlier relationship to both parents and her place in that household. She agreed, thus setting an oedipal focus for the work. What follows are excerpts from the first and sixth sessions. The therapist is male.

First Session.

P: Looking at things this way must be working because I've been anxious all week. I visited my gynecologist this week, and I was very angry at the pregnant women. My

husband and I talked about adoption and I felt guilty —
I felt I was cheating him — I also feel that I've been neu-
tered and cheated. I want a normal pregnancy and de-
livery.

T: Last week and now, you're talking a lot about having
to produce for men — your husband, your father, your
grandfather, and about the guilt you feel if you don't
produce.

P: Yes, but it was my father who took care of me. My
mother didn't get things right. I remember asking her
where babies come from and she said fairy dust. I asked
my father and he told me — he would come through for
me — of course, I couldn't believe that.

T: You couldn't believe what?

P: My parents doing it — sex seemed so dirty — I think I was
brought up to believe that — I don't know — when my
father came home from the hospital with a new baby,
each time — he looked so happy. I remember a dream
I wanted to tell you about. In the dream I'm having intercourse with my father and he whispers, "Don't tell
Mommy."

 I had that dream when I was a teenager, but it
stuck in my head. Sometimes I'd think, how could I
have a dream like that? It makes me disgusted, but it's
a great dream, isn't it?

T: It sounds like a very important dream for you — let's try
and understand it better.

P: Oh, it's an oedipal dream — shouldn't I be over that
phase by now?

T: By "understand" I meant how you felt in the dream,
and all of your feelings about it now.

P: I feel torn when I think of the dream, like I want to push
it away. It's like being afraid and being excited at the
same time.

T: The fear and the excitement — can you remember those
feelings toward your father?

P: Yes, sort of. I can get pleasure thinking of that dream. I think I never resolved my relationship with my father. When I was little I'd think — I do all the cleaning, take care of the kids — what do we need Mommy for? If she left I'd redecorate the house. But I don't think I really thought of Daddy in sexual terms, not that kind of excitement.

T: But isn't that what you're saying in your dream? That you want him sexually?

P: The dream says it all. I wanted all of him. I didn't think it was fair that I did all the work — and he — he wasn't fair with me — I want to resolve my relationship with my father. I really want a better relationship with him now. I'd like to be his daughter.

The above is the beginning of the first session in which the patient very readily reveals her oedipal wishes toward her father, her wish to be both sexual and primary. The therapist's initial intervention — guilt over a need to produce for men — moves her away from current and emotionally charged material about the visit to the gynecologist and into the agreed upon focus. The therapist believes that the patient's feelings of anger at pregnant women, of disappointment, and of being cheated can be dealt with in a more meaningful way after uncovering the unconscious oedipal feelings. The father side of the triangle is pursued because it seems predominant in the evaluation and because this material appears very close to the surface. The patient readily reveals material often considered to be well repressed in healthy individuals, a finding not uncommon in well-integrated patients of the simple oedipal type.

In the next four sessions a great deal of time is spent discussing the patient's feelings about her father, husband, and therapist and about pregnancy. The therapist believes that a therapeutic alliance has been developing. The transference is a father transference — a desire to please the therapist. No negative feelings toward the therapist have yet emerged, and the overall transference is positive. Several attempts to explore the patient's feelings toward her mother have proved unsuccessful. In the sixth session some of this uncovering takes place.

Sixth Session.

P: I've been thinking about my mother-in-law, why I feel so guilty about her. I had some bad thoughts while I was taking care of her.

T: Bad thoughts?

P: Yes. I'd think to myself, "she'd be better off dead. She can't do much for herself. She's helpless." I didn't think that often, but it made me very guilty.

T: Do you think part of the guilt was because—your wanting her dead was not just for her sake, but for your sake and your husband?

P: Yes, I wanted my husband more with me, more concerned about me, but I couldn't ask him for more with her so sick and I really thought maybe the stress from all of this caused it. I don't know, maybe I bring it on myself. Sometimes when I was pregnant I'd be upset enough to have palpitations. Maybe I did do it to myself.

T: There's no evidence your emotions caused the miscarriage, but your emotions certainly led to anxiety and worry while you were pregnant.

P: Underneath I felt very good, very proud of myself, very fulfilled. But it was like I couldn't let myself feel that.

T: Do you know why you couldn't let yourself feel good?

P: I think it had to do with my mother-in-law. It would be hard to feel good while she was sick and dying.

T: Your thoughts—that she'd be better off dead—what part did they play in this?

P: I think I punished myself for those thoughts. Somehow if she didn't feel good and I didn't feel good, it was okay.

T: What were you punishing yourself for?

P: Wanting her dead and wanting everything all right for me, my marriage good, and a baby.

T: How do you feel now, thinking about your feelings?

P: Not so bad. I didn't do anything to her. I just had the thoughts. I'm beginning to see it's not so bad to have thoughts, even ones like that.

T: Thoughts of wanting someone dead.

P: I can see now how they come about.

T: Do you feel part of you was angry at your mother-in-law? She took time and attention; you even thought she helped cause your miscarriage.

P: I was angry with her but I didn't want to see myself angry at someone sick and helpless.

T: Isn't there a parallel here with your feelings toward your mother? That it was hard to let yourself be angry with her?

P: Well with my mother-in-law it's all clearer; with my mother it's all more subconscious. I did have the fantasy that mother would just go away, but I'd push it out of my mind. I didn't think it was right to have those thoughts, wishing she was out of the picture.

T: What were the fantasies about your mother going away?

P: Well, she had heart trouble—maybe—Grandma said she had a heart murmur—I still don't know to this day if there is anything wrong with her heart or not. I never wished her dead—never—in fact, sometimes I'd be afraid she'd die, if she had heart trouble. What I wished was that she'd just go away.

T: Your wishes about her are very important for your understanding your own feelings. Can you remember any more about them?

P: Well, I'd think maybe she'll die, but I wouldn't take it all the way. I mean, I didn't wish she would die. In the fantasy she would just go away. Then most of the fantasy would be about me and Daddy. How I'd change the furniture. That he would be an adult with me. That I would listen to his problems at work—my mother never did—how I'd be important to him. I'm feeling very sad now, just thinking how hard it was to have a father — I had to fantasize to be close to him. That is sad.

T: I understand that you're sad about your relationship with your father, but could we get back to your feelings about your mother and your fantasy of getting her out of the way?

P: Well, I'd think sometimes she'd go to the West Indies — you know, sort of a Tahiti syndrome [sic] — she'd get fed up and just want a new life and go off — it was sort of crazy, thinking that about a woman who couldn't go to the corner deli — she couldn't even make out a check. You know if I was going to have a fantasy, it would have been easier to kill her — she couldn't cope by herself, it would be kinder for her to be dead.

T: That's a fantasy you allowed yourself to have with your mother-in-law.

P: I know. It's harder with my mother, I want to push my thoughts away. I was very angry with her. You know, she always said that I ruined her life. If I wasn't born she says she'd have been a famous actress. She said my birth ruined her career.

T: So there is a lot of anger between the two of you.

P: Um hum. I don't like to think about it. You're supposed to love your mother and that's not what I felt. I felt sorry for her and sick of her and other things I don't want to think about.

T: But all of those mixed things you think about her have powerful effects on what you think of yourself.

The patient concludes the session by talking more about her disappointment in her mother and about her fears that her mother is mentally ill.

In the above session the uncovering of her competitive and murderous feelings toward her mother are beginning. The therapist's main interventions are to keep her on focus and to support her as she begins to explore deeply painful feelings. So far the patient has not made one positive comment about her mother. This unremitting anger, disappointment, and fear lead the therapist to address issues of the patient's identification with her mother before proceeding to further uncovering. Usually uncovering does not proceed sequentially as shown in Table 1, Chapter 2. Frequently, some uncovering leads to a phase of working through and this in turn leads back to further uncovering. The working alliance is being promoted by attention to the focus and interest in the patient, as well as by precision and clarification. No major transference interpretations beyond the patient's need to please the therapist have been made thus far.

A Typical Beginning Uncovering in a Well-Motivated Patient: Andrew B.

Andrew B. is a married man of 35 whose major complaint is the inability to live up to his potential at work. The following are excerpts from the first two sessions following an initial evaluation. The therapist is female.

First Session.

P: I've been thinking about my evaluation interview. It's interesting I didn't remember that I had been close to my mother at any time. When we talked at the interview I remembered that we were close, but then very quickly we became antagonists. I changed allegiances from my mother to my father. I've had treatment before, but we never talked about my relationship to my mother. I want to understand that, although it's hard for me to talk about feelings.

T: It is important for you to look at your relationship with your mother, but there was another aspect of the problems that you agreed to work on. Do you remember what that was?

P: No. I was so surprised about my having been close to my mother before switching and siding with my father that that's all I've been thinking about .

T: You also agreed to explore your competitive feelings

with your father and how they related to your feelings for your mother and your switch in allegiance.

P: Yes. I had forgotten that. In my past treatment I did a lot of work on my anger toward my father. I think that's why I forgot. The feelings about my mother were new and seemed important. I know I would be better than my father at work, but I just can't do it. I often struggle in my head with an image of my father that's really not like him. I see him as much harsher than he was. I don't know why that is.

Since the first interview I've tried to think of affectionate times with my mother, but when I think of her I think of how emotional and irrational she is and it's hard to imagine that I was ever close to that. Although I did remember that when I was sick we'd get close.

T: What do you mean by close? What did the two of you do when you were sick?

P: Well, she'd stay with me a lot, cook me special foods, read to me, and yeah, there was something a little embarrassing. My mother would sponge bathe me, in bed, all over, even when I was older. Actually, I remember I often pretended to be sick to be with her.

T: She must have been very special if you stayed home to be with her.

P: Yeah, I guess she was. There was something else too. My father wasn't good about feelings; he wasn't sentimental or anything like that. And my mother was all feelings. I used to remember her birthday and all special occasions and do something for her. I remember thinking I was giving her what my father couldn't give. In fact, my giving her things was almost a family joke. My mother really loved it.

The patient then goes on to talk more about his father. He describes an absence of closeness, except for designated times when his father would "teach" him something. These times were frequent, two or three times a week. They were a nightmare for the patient, who felt that his father used these times to bully him. He was never physically abused, but subjected to harsh criticism and constant testing. He says that he is angry at himself for allowing it to happen. He also says that he was angry at his mother for not intervening.

Second Session.

P: I was feeling sick this week. My back hurt, but I guess it's nothing (long pause with no response from therapist). I remembered something painful this week. My mother rejected me. That's how the change came about. She stepped back from me when I became sexual. I remember exactly when it happened. She was going to bathe me when I was sick and she saw that I had pubic hair. She put everything away and was never close to me again. Oh, I don't know, maybe I stepped back then too. I really don't know who stepped back, maybe we both did. Sex was just not allowed in my family. It was too scary. It still is scary to me, too uncontrolled. Yet I was interested in sex. I would hide sex magazines in my room. My brother was openly interested in sex; he was different from the rest of my family. I'd hide these magazines and be in terror that my brother would find them and tell everyone my secret.

T: Just what was your secret that had you in such terror?

P: My interest in sex. I know it doesn't make sense. My brother was open about sex and nothing happened, yet I felt I had to hide my interest. It's funny because I really was in terror and yet I really knew nothing would happen. It doesn't make sense. There was something about my interest in sex that I just knew had to be hidden. I used to hide in my room and masturbate. This is interesting—when I masturbated I had a particular fantasy: somebody—I don't know who—a man—wouldn't pay attention to me—he thought I could be overlooked, but in my fantasy I killed him. I'd shoot him for not paying attention to me and that got me sexually excited and I'd come. That fantasy gave me great pleasure, but somehow it also made me know that all my feelings should be hidden.

The patient continues the session, presenting variations on the fantasy, which occurred until after college. He talks of the gun being power and of using the image of the gun to relax when he was tense. He claims that for the past several years the gun fantasy has not occurred, that it had bothered him, and that he had purposely taught himself other ways of relaxing. He continues by reiterating the mismatch between his terror about doing something wrong and the fact that he was never punished for things he did wrong. He says that his parents were not sufficiently concerned about him. He ends the session by asking the therapist for suggestions as to what to think about next week. The therapist does not comply.

From an initial evaluation and two sessions we see a clear unfolding of the patient's oedipal conflicts. From an early position of not being able to imagine being close to his mother, he recovers significant memories of their closeness, or of his need to be special to her, and of the frustration of the oedipal wish at puberty. His secret wish, his sexual desire for his mother coupled with his desire to murder and displace his father, is revealed in his masturbatory fantasies. The patient is clearly working and the therapist has been relatively inactive in the sessions. The therapist did clarify the focus when the patient left out the agreement about competitive feeling. Much more has been revealed in these sessions than has been explicitly dealt with as yet. The patient is also aware of this and he continually points out the discrepancy between his feelings and reality as he remembers it. This acknowledgment is another sign of his working on the problem. The patient buys closeness with his mother by taking a sick or castrated position. In the second session we see him reevoking this with his therapist. The therapist has chosen not to confront him with this posture, but neither does the therapist gratify his request for attention or direction. The above excerpt is presented to show a rather typical beginning uncovering in a well-motivated patient. As might have been predicted from the first session in which the patient "forgets" half the focus, this patient has great difficulty in acknowledging and reexperiencing his competitive feelings for his father.*

Editor's note: The patient's reverting to passivity and dependency by asking the therapist for suggestions can be viewed here as a defensive regression that directly follows the emergence of sexual and aggressive ideation. Paying attention to the sequence of material reveals impulse, anxiety, and defense. The castrated position

Uncovering in a Situation of
Isolation of Affect: Leo C.

The following is an example of a patient who presents a somewhat more difficult problem in uncovering.

Leo C. is a married, highly successful businessman in his early fifties. He states that he is happily married and has a good relationship with his two children, both of whom are in college. His presenting problem is free-floating and situational anxiety of four years' duration. This began when his employer asked him to take a particular assignment that he did not want to accept and yet felt unable to refuse. Notable in his history in terms of suggesting an oedipal focus are the following: memories of an early closeness to his mother and feelings that this closeness was lost when he was 5 or 6 years old plus a feeling that his mother worshipped his father and his recollection of being continually jealous about her preference. He describes his father as very tough and strong and his relationship to his father as one of fear and anxiety mixed with a desire to please. He has had numerous prior attempts at psychotherapy; all ended prematurely and were unsuccessful. The patient is highly intelligent and prone to intellectualization. It is hypothesized that the patient's anxiety has been triggered by an activation of his competitive oedipal conflicts in relationship to his boss. The therapist also feels that the patient's marked isolation of affect is a defense against strong oedipally derived sexual and aggressive feelings. The patient was asked if his feelings when his boss asked him to take the assignment four years before were similar to his feelings of fearing his father and yet wanting to please him. The patient feels that the feelings were quite similar and that many of his feelings toward his boss, and doing things for the boss, are similar to feelings toward his father. The therapist reiterated a connection between his current performance anxiety and performance anxiety with his father. The patient was asked if he was interested in exploring his anxiety as a function of

can be understood as a compromise formation that (1) buys closeness with the mother and gratifies the oedipal wish, (2) wards off punishment by the father (the therapist), (3) constitutes a self-punishment for the wish, alleviating guilt, and (4) renders the sexual and aggressive impulses harmless.

his earlier relation to his mother and father. He agreed that seemed a useful way of proceeding. Thus, the contract was set.

What follows are excerpts from the first four sessions following the evaluation. The therapist is male.

First Session.

p: I'd like to talk about my feelings when I'm anxious, particularly when I'm anxious at work. I feel that other people can sense my anxiety and I don't like that. I don't want that.

t: Last time we agreed to try and understand your anxiety and your feelings about it in terms of your early relationship with your parents.

p: Yes, I remember. I've been thinking about them. When I was bad—or when my father thought I was bad—I was put in a closet. This was when I was small, before I was in school. The darkness frightened me. When I was 13 I remember my parents locking my sister in a closet. It's very vivid. Her thumb got caught in the door and she began to scream. They opened the door and her thumb was hanging off. My father started to beat himself when he saw it. He hit himself and he hit me. (The patient looks slightly anxious. The above story is told with little affect.)

I had night fears. They were very bad. I was sent to camp. It was very competitive. The counselors hit me with a paddle if they thought I did anything wrong. I was sent away for six years, although I hated it and didn't want to go. The kids there didn't like me much. I wasn't good at sports. I was afraid of the kids mostly—that's interesting—now I'm afraid of those in authority.

t: You've described a number of fears of performing in front of males, and they all sound very much like your feelings when you performed in front of your father.

p: I was always anxious with my father. My father didn't want a son—he wanted full attention from my mother.

He didn't want anything that would take attention away from him.

T: It sounds like there was a strong competition between you and your father for your mother's attention. Certainly, he openly competed with you and you must have wanted to compete with him.

P: I didn't compete with him. I know I withdrew from competition, but I wasn't always that way. I used to be wild before I was 5 or 6. In first grade there was a possibility that I'd be left back. My mother took me away for the summer and taught me to read. My father came up weekends, so he only saw her on weekends. After that summer I was sent away.

T: How did it feel to be alone with your mother that summer?

P: I can't say. I just have vague memories.

T: As you talked about it, there was an expression of sadness, as if there was something pleasant in being with your mother that summer, and then you lost something when you went to camp.

P: I know I lost something. I have an image, a memory of my mother falling down.

The above is the major portion of the first session. The therapist's first intervention is to reiterate the focus. The therapist feels that the patient's sense of vulnerability in having his anxiety visible will be more fruitfully explored after the roots of this problem are uncovered. Additionally, the therapist is reminding the patient of the particular way in which they have agreed to work. The first session offers evidence confirming the oedipal hypothesis. There is the castration memory of his sister and her dangling thumb, and the harsh punishment following a summer when he has won mother for a time. The concept of competition with father for mother is introduced by the therapist and the patient's associations, i.e., the summer with mother followed by his years in camp, are in line with this intervention. The most striking feature of the entire session is the patient's isolation of affect. This alerts the therapist to the possibility of an intellectual experience with the patient which, like previous therapies, will not be useful.

Second Session.

P: What we talked about last week was theoretical and interesting. I know some about my past fears and even about how my childhood connects to the present, but there's no emotional connection.

T: I agree that it's very important for you to experience your feelings. When you talk with me about yourself it feels as if we're both talking about someone else.

P: When I'm with my father I can't have any emotions. When I'm apart from my father I can be angry.

T: Is your experience with me like being with your father? You don't show feelings with either of us.

P: NO.

The patient's "no" is followed by a long speech berating the father, and the session contains more data about the patient's anxiety and fears of punishment. What is most encouraging about the session is the patient's concern with his lack of affect. This then is, to some degree, ego-alien and there is agreement between patient and therapist that the material must be experienced as well as talked about. The patient is disturbed by his anger at the therapist, as this is the emotion he singles out as possible when father is not present. The therapist introduces the father transference, which is evident, but does not push the patient or argue with the patient after the patient's denial. This transference manifestation will come up again and as the working alliance gets stronger, the patient is expected to be better able to acknowledge the transference, including his desire to berate, belittle, and best the therapist, as shown by his berating of his father at the end of the session.

Third Session.

P: I've been thinking about this process. Where are the feelings?

T: You're here with me right now. There must be feelings about being here with me.

P: I want to be liked by you and by others. I try to please you.

T: I know that you want to be in touch with your feelings with me, but that's difficult for you. You keep running away from your feelings in here. What are the feelings that you have toward me that you think would stop me from liking you?

P: You'll see that I'm weak and embarrassed.

T: Weak, embarrassed. It sounds like a competition between us, with you losing. What about your feelings of winning or showing me up?

P: No, I'm afraid of losing. I want to please you. I don't want to lose.

T: You're talking like I'm your father, out to embarrass and humiliate you if I get a chance.

P: I see what you're saying. It's true. That connects with my work. I'm afraid, in a way, of everyone at work. I needn't be so afraid. If I make a mistake they're not going to pull any medals off me. They're not out to embarrass me. I just feel that way.

The session continues on the theme of competition, and competition with father for mother is introduced. The patient uses this to go off focus and compares men and women. The therapist brings him back.

T: Let's go back. We were talking about your competition with men.

P: You know I'm a success. I'm good at work. I'm good with my wife. My kids are in good shape. I wonder why I got so upset four years ago and stayed that way.

T: I know that you're a success. What do you think happened four years ago that got you so anxious?

The patient then explores his conflict between pleasing his boss and saying no. The competitive father transference is being managed in a way in which the patient can be successful without retaliation. The patient focuses on fear of losing in competition, while the therapist is pointing out his additional fears of winning.

Fourth Session.

P: I've been thinking about humiliation. If I could disasso-
ciate my anxiety from humiliation and competition from
humiliation, I'd feel much better. Whenever I competed
with my father it ended in my being humiliated. There's
a funny paradox. Sometimes I just do things well. Other
times I try, and the more I try, the less I do. You know,
in most games I just won't compete. I'll play if they
don't keep score.

T: Can you remember a situation when you competed with
your father?

P: It's hard. It wasn't really out in the open. Sometimes
I'd punish myself before he punished me. When I didn't
do well at school, I'd come home and hide in the closet.
If I broke a lamp, Mother would say, "hide it before
Daddy sees it."

T: So your mother took your side in a way. She tried to
protect you.

P: Yes, she was very different from my father. When he
wasn't around, I got a lot from her: attention, care,
love.

T: When you remember back to being alone with your
mother, the attention, care, and the love, do you have
any memories of sexual feelings?

P: I can't remember it, but I remember times when it must
have been there; sometimes in the bath when she'd touch
me there. I must have been stimulated. I can't remember
the feeling.

  I remember once when I was 4 or 5, friends came
to the house. They had a daughter my age, a little older.
She slept in my bed. My parents got a teenage boy to
act as a babysitter. We were jumping up and down and
having fun. Then the boy told us to stop. I picked up
a rock and threw it at him — hard — it left a gash on his
forehead.

T: That's an interesting memory. Can you remember your
feelings then?

P: A lot of excitement. I remember the excitement of jumping up and down, yelling. We were having fun. I was excited when I threw the rock. It horrifies me now, but then I liked it. I think I was showing off, too, showing how strong I was, that no one could stop me. I thought it was funny. I don't feel good talking about this.

T: What's happening with you right now?

P: It's horrible to look at myself then. A few years later, with that same girl, we were playing again, yelling, excited. I threw a toy at her and hit her. I got very frightened. I thought I was going to jail. I really thought I was.

T: What's the horror about?

P: That I would get too excited, that I could hurt someone and not care — get that carried away.

T: When you were talking earlier about competition, you said you were wild when you were young. Then things changed and you were different.

P: That's true. Now it's very hard to be aggressive, even when I should be. I keep thinking, "What will they think? What will they say?"

T: You're talking about retaliation for your aggression — if you hit, you'll get hit back.

P: My father would hit, even if I didn't start it. That made me very frightened to hit back. I want to compete and I want to be good.

T: What does "to be good" mean?

P: To not want to hurt anyone.

T: Did you want to hurt your father?

P: Logically I must have, but I can't feel it.

T: Do you have any memories of getting back at your father? You have vivid memories of his punishing you, hitting you, putting you in closets.

P: Those memories only bring back my fear of him, not anger, although it must have been there.

T: One of the complaints in our work is your absence of

feelings. When a feeling is very strong, such as anger against me or your father, don't you think that you block it out?

P: Yes, I have a sense that I do that.

T: When you were talking about jumping on the bed and the excitement, the showing off, you said you were horrified that you could be so carried away.

P: Yes. I feel much better when I'm in control, when I can compete without competing, if you know what I mean. I remember watching a TV story. Kids were playing ball. The coach told them to get tougher, beat each other up if they have to. One kid just walked off the field. I want to be that kid.

T: I can understand what you're saying, but aren't you talking about walking away from that wild boy on the bed who threw the rock? About walking away from parts of yourself?

P: To be able to walk away — it would be handy.

The above is the major part of the fourth session. The memory of the girl and the babysitter contain the core oedipal dilemma. The oedipal wishes are expressed in derivative form. There is the sexual excitement with the girl, a memory stimulated by questions of sexual excitement toward mother, and the destruction of the interfering male babysitter (father). The patient is beginning to be in touch with a fear of his own feelings. The sexual excitement leads him to an out-of-control destructive feeling, which disgusts him. The transference is still that of a compliant son to his father. The therapist has strengthened the alliance by being able to hear and tolerate the patient's feelings. He also continues to accept the patient's strength without becoming competitive and in pointing out the patient's expectation of a competitive retaliation.†

The main point to be made with this vignette is that uncovering must go on at an experiential level and that even in brief therapy one does not short-circuit the process by giving the patient an unex-

---

†_Editor's note_: One might note that the "corrective emotional experience" contributes to good outcome (Alexander and French, 1946).

perienced cognitive view of his problems. The competitive elements with this patient become more available as treatment proceeds. These elements and the affect generated in the transference lead to a return to father in a later session.

References

Alexander, F., and French, T. (1946). *Psychoanalytic Psychotherapy*. New York: Ronald Press.

Davanloo, H. (1980). *Short-Term Dynamic Psychotherapy*. New York: Jason Aronson.

Greenson, R. (1967). *The Technique and Practice of Psychoanalysis*. New York: International Universities Press.

Malan, D. (1976a). *The Frontier of Brief Psychotherapy*. New York: Plenum Press.

_____. (1976b). *Towards the Validation of Dynamic Psychotherapy*. New York: Plenum Press.

Sifneos, P. (1979). *Short-Term Dynamic Psychotherapy*. New York: Plenum Press.

Stolorow, R., and Lachmann, F. (1980). *Psychoanalysis of Developmental Arrests*. New York: International Universities Press.

Chapter 8

WORKING THROUGH

ARNOLD WINSTON, M.D.
MANUEL TRUJILLO, M.D.

As the uncovering phase progresses through the use of confrontation, clarification, and interpretation, the therapy gradually moves into the working-through phase. Generally, there is not a clear demarcation between these phases, and uncovering may continue throughout the treatment. In the same way, working through will often continue into the resolution and termination phases and at times even after therapy is over.

Working Through Defined

In this book we conceptualize working through using Greenson's (1967) formulation:

> Working through refers to a complex set of procedures and processes which occur after an insight has been given. The analytic work which makes it possible for an insight to lead to change is the work of working through. It refers in the main to the repetitive, progressive and elaborate explorations of the resistances which prevent an insight from leading to change. . . . A variety of circular processes are set in motion by working through in which insight, memory and behavior change influence each other.

In short-term dynamic psychotherapy it is necessary that the "circular processes" of working through be rapidly mobilized. Insight, memory, and behavior change interact with one another but must be accompanied by affect to be therapeutically effective. Each major conflict should be worked through in a number of areas. This can be illustrated with the following clinical example.

A 37-year-old man in a middle-management position is enmeshed in conflict with a number of men, including his boss, father, brother, and friends. In these relationships he behaves in either a passive, self-effacing manner or is inappropriately angry and self-destructive. For working through to be effective, it is necessary for this conflict to be carefully explored and analyzed in relation to all of these men and, most importantly, in the therapeutic relationship. Omission of any of this from the working-through process often leads to only a partial resolution of the conflict and sometimes to no therapeutic change at all.

Just as a conflict must be worked through in a number of areas, it must be linked to other conflicts. For example, if the nuclear conflict consists of rage toward the father and a wish for an exclusive relationship with the mother, these two elements must be brought together and not allowed to remain in "separate compartments."

Steps of the Working-Through Process

The working-through process contains a number of steps (Table 1, Chapter 2) that must be accomplished during short-term psychotherapy. First, the wish to have the opposite-sex parent sexually and to be the preferred object must be given up. The patient must see how these wishes enter into his everyday life, and how they apply to the transference situation. This will often be manifested in the patient's everyday life by a refusal to replace the opposite-sex parent with a suitable current love object. Eventually, identification with the opposite-sex parent must be acknowledged without the fear of loss of gender identity.

With the same-sex parent, the wish to defeat in competition, displace, and murder should be renounced. Often the patient has reacted to this wish to murder with guilt and self-sabotage, resulting in interference with achievement or outright failure. Working this through often enables the patient to compete in a healthy and vigorous manner, which can lead to a higher level of achievement. As these wishes are renounced, identification with the same-sex parent should be seen by the patient as having taken place without danger to the patient's own ego ideal.

Straightforward Unfolding with the Uncomplicated Oedipal Focus: Sandra G.

Again, we begin the clinical examples with a relatively uncomplicated case, that of Sandra G., whose history was presented in the previous chapter on uncovering. (See pages 120–127.) The patient's treatment unfolds in a straightforward manner through the uncovering phase and into the working through. What emerges is an uncomplicated oedipal situation with strong positive and erotic feelings for her father. She feels angry toward and superior to her mother and expresses fantasies containing death wishes for her mother. The following clinical material is taken from treatment session 9, which is well into the working-through phase.

> P: I have a cold. It really gets me angry to get sick so soon after just getting over another cold. I guess I want mothering. Then I don't have to do certain jobs, like housework. I don't like to do housework—it gets me angry. You know it connects to the past—my having to do the housework; my mother couldn't do it. I've always been better able to cope than my mother. In my mind I've been saying that I'm a better wife than you are but I didn't feel comfortable about that. Now with tennis, when I played with my husband, I felt that I was as good as him, but I always lost. The last time we played, I thought about the issue of conquest—with my mother, with him, and I started to win. Something in me was changing.
>
> T: You felt more comfortable winning.
>
> P: Yes. It made me remember when I was young. I was

a good speller, but I never wanted to go into spelling bees. I think I would lose on purpose. I was afraid of being in public. Even now when I have to talk at parent workshops . . . I don't like public speaking, making presentations. I get nervous and obsess about it.

T: Feeling anxious about being in public, exposing or exhibiting yourself in these situations, in school and now as an adult.

P: It's interesting that you said exhibiting yourself publicly. I would never exhibit myself in front of my father the way my mother did. Am I afraid of my feelings or afraid of his feelings?

T: Well, let's look into that.

P: I didn't want him looking at me. I remember feeling that he shouldn't be thinking what he might be thinking.

T: What did you imagine he might be thinking?

P: Noting my figure . . . if I'm wearing a bra or not wearing one. He shouldn't be noticing that.

T: He shouldn't be noticing that?

P: I'm not his wife. He should be a parent.

T: But you have said that you would be a better wife for him, and we know you have had sexual feelings for your father — the dream about wanting your father sexually and having sexual intercourse with him.

P: Yes. I was suppressing my feelings by saying he was interested in me and not me in him. I certainly was interested in him. I did the housework, cleaning for him, so he would notice me, not my mother. Yet he never really turned to me. She was the one who really had him.

T: So ultimately she was more successful with your father than you were. You did the housework, but she had him sexually.

P: Yes, I can see even now that I compete with her for his attention. And when I was younger, I even wanted to be a model like my mother was. Then I could feel pretty, thin, have a good shape, and wear nice clothes.

T: Good shape in what way?

P: Be thin, but not have to diet. Then I realized that models are flat-chested and I didn't want that.

T: And your mother, what did she look like?

P: Thin, not flat-chested, medium.

T: How do you compare physically to your mother?

P: We are similar in a lot of ways: same legs, I'm thinner than she. I felt better than her because I was thinner. She had a pretty face; I wanted to wear makeup the way she did. But you know, I wanted her to love me. She never said that she loved me. I feel sad about that, but angry with her also because of that and because of the housework. I'm having palpitations now as I talk about this. I feel very upset.

T: Palpitations, upset. You feel anger toward your mother and then become anxious and have palpitations.

P: I have the feeling of being denied my childhood. I can see now that my anger and competing with my mother enters into everything — speaking in public, tennis — but these things are also ways of exposing myself. My fear of exposing and exhibiting myself to my father by wearing low-cut clothes also inhibits me from speaking in public. You know, my getting these colds, like the one I have now, it's really a need for punishment.

T: Punishment?

P: Punishment for wanting to take my mother's place, for wanting to get rid of her, wishing her dead; but having a cold is also a way of my wishing to be cared for.

T: Cared for by whom?

P: By you. I want you to be a parent, a mother or father. Being sick is being helpless and cared for.

T: You want to give me the message that you are helpless and need me.

P: I want your help and attention, but I want you to feel I've made progress. You would feel good about my progress and think well of me, that I'm moving along, fighting to get better.

T: You wȧnt me to notice you, to see that you are better, as you wanted your father to notice that you were important and give you attention, and to say that you're better than your mother.

P: I did expect that from my father, but I realize now, how could he say that? He would have had to admit that his wife wasn't adequate.

The patient then goes on to discuss her realization that her father could not tell her she was better than his wife and that this was really her wish. Additional angry feelings emerge toward her mother for standing in her way. These are linked to her mother-in-law. Her angry and ambivalent feelings toward her mother-in-law whom she nursed before her death are explored, and the two triangles of mother-in-law–husband–patient and mother-father-patient are examined.

Since this is a patient with a symptom neurosis with a relatively uncomplicated oedipal focus, as opposed to a character neurosis, the working-through phase unfolds in a fairly straightforward manner. The oedipal conflict is worked through and linked to current difficulties. On sequential examination of these sessions, one sees that first the patient brings up her sexual wishes for her father. These are brought up in a clear and direct manner after the therapist interprets some of the defenses against these wishes. The therapist then connects these directly to the patient's frankly sexual dream about her father. The other side of the oedipal triangle soon appears. The patient's ambivalent feelings toward her mother, whom she wanted to emulate and whom she yearned for, emerges, along with the patient's negative and angry thoughts and feelings. These are then clarified and the connection made between the patient's emerging anger toward her mother and the palpitations arising during the sessions. In addition, some of her phobic symptoms are linked to her angry and negative feelings toward her mother and her positive sexual feelings toward her father.

This work then leads to the notion of the patient's punishing herself for wanting to get rid of her mother, which leads to transference feelings for the therapist. The therapist is then able to connect these feelings toward himself to the patient's positive feelings for her father.

Finally, links are made to the onset of the patient's symptoms when she began to care for her dying mother-in-law. Caring for her mother-in-law, whom she saw as a competitor for her husband, ignited the unresolved oedipal conflict in this woman. Clarification of this and the linking of the triangle of mother-father-patient with the triangle of husband–mother-in-law–patient helps to further the working-through process.

Breakthrough of Isolated Affect: Leo C.

The next clinical example is a continuation of the case of the 50-year-old businessman from the previous chapter. The session begins 15 minutes late because the therapist was involved in an emergency with another patient. The patient begins by talking about a young woman trainee from his office. He has had a chance-meeting with her on the subway and found himself looking at her. He was concerned that she might be thinking that he wanted to pick her up. During the next several minutes two interruptions (telephone calls) occur, lasting at least five minutes each. The patient continues as if nothing has happened, picking up where he had left off. He goes on to say that perhaps he has thought about picking her up, since he has no way of knowing what she was thinking.

T: (*Interrupting*) I'm interrupting you because it's striking that we started 15 minutes late because I was late, and then we were interrupted twice by phone calls that took some time, and yet you go on as if nothing happened.

P: Well, I understand, you're a doctor. People call and there are emergencies.

T: It's curious that you are so understanding. All these interruptions!

P: Well, I understand. It's not your fault. I'm not upset.

T: Upset? It seems to me that my being late and all the interruptions might have produced a great deal of feelings on your part.

P: I know I should have felt irritated or even angry, but I didn't, so I can't say that.

T: You can't say that?

P: Well, it's a strategy I use from way back. I hardly ever allow myself to get angry, and that's especially true here with you.

T: Last session you said that you wanted me to like you. What do you think would happen here if you got angry?

P: If I get angry, I have a feeling that you'll be disapproving of me.

T: Disapproving?

P: Well, if I get angry with you, you might get upset with me or angry with me, not like me, very much the way I felt toward my father. I never allowed myself to get angry with him, no matter what happened or what he said. I wanted him to care about me, to love me.

The session continues on this theme, and the conflict toward his father and boss are clarified in terms of his anger and competitive feelings as opposed to his need to please his father and be loved by him. At the end of this session the patient states that he will be on vacation for the next two weeks and is thinking about not coming in for his therapy sessions. The therapist replies that this is the patient's decision, but that the patient will be responsible financially for the visits. The patient promptly replies that he will come in for the next two sessions.

Thus far, the work in therapy has progressed fairly well through the uncovering and into the working-through process. However, the patient, in earlier sessions, has recognized that it is difficult for him to attach feelings to what he is talking about and that the therapy has been more intellectual than emotional.

In this session the therapist attempted to take advantage of a naturally occurring situation that should have provoked a great deal of feeling on the part of the patient. However, the patient was able to deal with this primarily on an intellectual level. His fear of father (therapist) in terms of loss of love and retaliation begins to surface. The therapist clarifies the transference situation, and the patient is able to make a parent-therapist link. The focus is maintained on the father side of the oedipal triangle. The next session extends this work emotionally and in greater detail into many areas of the patient's life.

P: At the end of the last session I was debating about coming here, since I'm on vacation. You said I would have to pay for the sessions either way.

T: What was your feeling about that?

P: I felt you were irritated with me, but I was irritated and angry with you. It's not fair. You never told me about the policy for missed sessions.

T: It's interesting that you didn't bring up your anger about the policy last time.

P: I felt if I did it would be an irritant to the relationship. You said something and I shouldn't question it. I guess it's like a little boy in a submissive position.

T: So what you did was to put yourself in a submissive position rather than express your angry feelings.

P: I'm sensitive to you, to the other person, if I get irritated or angry. It's like my anxiety in front of groups or with my boss. It's the same kind of sensitivity. I always felt the other person could retaliate, like my father putting me into the closet, or that I would be humiliated making a presentation.

T: So not getting angry because you feared retaliation from me, as with your father, or humiliation, as with your boss, are connected.

P: Yes, the fear of being hurt and humiliated is devastating. I get paralyzed. You know it was even worse when I was in school or camp, with other kids; I was always trying to please. The other kids at camp called me an asshole, yet I continued to go to camp for seven years. I never complained to my parents. In college it was the same thing. I was looked down on. They played all sorts of pranks on me in the dormitory. No one chose me as a roommate for the sophmore year. I just took it all.

T: So you had difficulty asserting yourself, getting angry with your father, and then with kids at school, camp, and college. You make yourself passive rather than risk standing up for yourself and competing.

P: I was sensitive to being hurt if I stood up for myself. At work I've had the fantasy that if I messed up at a presentation, the boss would rip off my epaulets like a military sort of thing.

T: Sort of a castration. You mentioned a few sessions ago, when talking about your father and your boss, having a surgery fantasy and an actual appendectomy when you were 6 years old. It sounds as if you are actually frightened of a physical hurt.

P: I never really felt that I would be hurt or castrated. I always go back to the closet issue with my father. But I wasn't physically hurt.

T: That's true. But what about the experience you told me about, your sister being locked in the closet by your father, the door closing on her thumb, and her thumb hanging off as a result.

P: I see that. (*Appears quite moved.*) My father could have done that to me, especially if I stood up for myself.

T: And you feel I could if you get angry with me. So it was difficult for you, and you had to wait a week to tell me that you were angry with me.

P: My being so fearful, afraid to let people know I'm angry, is reminiscent of the fear at my Bar Mitzvah, as I've told you before. I was afraid my voice would crack, everyone would hear it. It's like the anxiety I feel in front of my boss when I have to make a presentation.

T: In other words, your anxiety in making presentations is related to your fear of getting angry with your father, schoolmates, and me. You're afraid to be assertive, to speak up, to be angry for fear of being retaliated against and being hurt.

The masochistic and passive posture of the patient is clearly demonstrated in this last session. However, it should be noted that the patient did achieve a great deal of success in his work, at school, and in his marriage. He was able, to a certain extent, to be active and assertive in these situations. His passivity, therefore, was seen as defensive and of oedipal origin rather than as characterological. The patient was defending against competitive, aggressive, and murderous impulses toward his father and his fear of retaliation. As the patient becomes more comfortable with his aggressive feelings, he can be assertive and less passive.

This is the beginning of the resolution process (see the next chapter), with the removal of fear from assertive actions.

Working Through Loss Issues and Defensive Homosexuality: Larry G.

Larry G. is a 30-year-old single, unemployed male who entered psychotherapy during an episode of depression related to his impending loss of a relationship with his girlfriend, with whom he established a passive, dependent and unfulfilling relationship. In addition to this depression, his emotional difficulties include a pervasive sense of emptiness and chronically low self-esteem; lack of productivity and assertiveness as indicated by his dropping out of high school and finding himself frequently unemployed; and difficulties in his relationships with women, including sexual problems. He has an extensive history of homosexuality and expresses fears of sexual intercourse with women. With his girlfriend he tends to be passive, submissive, and masochistic. He is unable to assert himself and frequently finds himself exploited and resentful. His relationships with his peers, especially males, are also impaired. He feels inferior and has to put distance between himself and his friends, which leaves him totally isolated. He has a very poor relationship with his family. He is afraid of and distant from his father and is excessively involved with his mother, feeling guilty about his inability to comply with many of her demands. As an example, he feels vaguely anxious and guilty when she voices complaints of loneliness and feels compelled to spend a lot of his free time with her, "making her feel better about herself."

The patient has enjoyed a very close relationship with his mother. He cherishes an early memory in which he was in the basement of his house together with his brother and mother during a civil defense exercise. He vividly remembers with great pleasure the closeness and affection and the intense feelings provoked in him by the closeness to his mother. The early relationship with his father was also a good one, but in the patient's mind it was almost completely replaced by a bitter, prolonged struggle in which he feared and avoided close contact with his father during childhood, adolescence, and early adulthood. This, in turn, mobilized in him deep feelings of craving for a closer relationship with his father.

These early, warm relations with his mother, markedly eroticized, became the focus of a very intense oedipal rivalry. To preserve this sense of closeness, he distanced himself from his father and established very competitive relationships with his brothers and sisters. His anger and distance from his father, in addition to the father's own difficulties in communicating with his children, prevented the development of sublimatory identification with his father and successful separation from his mother. Sibling rivalry made it difficult for him to use the often beneficial support network of brothers and sisters. As a result, he became passively depressed, angry, and isolated. Becoming a "cripple" is now the main stance used with his father and his only claim to the perpetuation of a selective relationship with his mother. As long as he takes the position of a "beaten man," he can ward off his oedipal fears of his father and neutralize his strivings for his mother. As a result, few areas of personal functioning remain outside of this set of conflicts. The treatment of this patient is completed in a total of 15 sessions, over the course of 4½ months. The psychotherapeutic focus is established during both the initial evaluation and the first treatment interview. As the patient reveals his current sadness at the loss of his girlfriend, this is linked to a very intense early attachment to his mother, and the memory emerges of being close to his mother's body in the basement of his house shortly after World War II began. As this early, intense, sexualized longing for his mother is explored, unconscious oedipal fears are also mobilized. He states, "As a child I wondered what it was to have your cock cut off."

In the vignettes that follow we have an opportunity to see within the transference the appearance of an oedipal focus as well as a loss focus. As the patient experiences, in reference to the therapist, both the fear of castration and the fear of abandonment, the therapeutic relationship becomes more solid and resistances diminish. The therapeutic alliance becomes firm after active exploration of both foci.

The process of change starts to appear in session 6, as working through begins. In this session the patient starts by talking about his fear that the therapist will not be there for the session, or that for some reason the session will not be possible. He indicates that he feels guilty in relation to the therapist, that he feels "like a little kid." It may have something to do, he says, with his experience on Saturday in which he and Joey, his former homosexual partner, went to visit his mother. On his way back to the city he stopped at his brother's house and decided to spend the night there, since it was already quite late. His brother and brother's girlfriend spent the night in the bedroom, while the patient and Joey went to sleep in the living room. He woke up in the middle of the night with some anxiety and started "messing around with Joey."

T: You started messing around with him.

P: I did it for a couple of minutes with his cock and things like that. I did it for a couple of minutes and then I said, you know, I just got confused. "I don't know what the hell I'm doing." And just said "sorry" and that was it. I felt badly about it.

T: You invited Joey to go with you to your mother's house? (*P: Right*.) Now, why?

P: Because my mother's doing work down there and he's an architect. He's a designer and he would help my mother. That's the premise.

T: Is there anything else?

P: There probably is, and I don't know what it is. So you're going to have to help me. I have no idea.

T: Well, you said too quickly. "There probably is." And you smile, and . . .

P: That I wanted to tell my mother that I was gay. All right? Is that what you want to hear?

T: No, I want to hear whatever comes to your mind.

P: That's what came to mind.

T: If, indeed, you had erotic thoughts toward your mother, as we had been discussing . . .

P: It's a safety valve, right? A safety valve. I tell my dad, "Hey, you don't got to worry about me and Mom."

T: Right. You don't have to worry about me and Mom. That's correct.

Following this therapeutic interaction, the patient recalls how he used to have many nightmares as a child and get into bed between his mother and father. He remembers that at that time he used to have the fantasy of having his "cock cut off."

This clinical vignette signals a deepening of the working-through process. The patient allows himself increased contact with his unconscious processes, and both of his Saturday activities (going to his mother's house and the event at his brother's house that night) can be seen as "reparative work." Through these two activities the patient manages to reactivate a deeply felt core conflict in a very vivid manner. His defensive homosexuality reappeared in relation to the triangle with his brother and his brother's girlfriend. The insight that the patient derived from this experience had a very vivid impact on his ego. For the first time he clearly understood how his unconscious mind determined many of his feelings and actions. The patient also made available to the therapist an abundance of conflictual material, enabling connections between the past, the present, and the transference in an affectively charged atmosphere. The patient also showed in this vignette that his ego was capable of renouncing the homosexual wishes, which were defensive in nature.

In sessions 8 and 9 there is intensive therapeutic work at the level of the transference. The patient experiences feelings of anger toward the therapist, accompanied by intense anxiety. At the beginning of session 8, he states that he is very angry at the therapist, who has kept him waiting five or six minutes beyond the starting time of the session. In his next association he indicates that for the last two or three sessions, he compulsively has to go to the bathroom just before the beginning of the session and that he experiences a sensation of tension in his penis. Following this the patient becomes very competitive with the therapist, and these competitive feelings are linked with his feeling of castration in the transference. This theme is followed through in the next two or three sessions, and the patient becomes progressively more comfortable with his angry, competitive, and jealous feelings toward the therapist.

The following vignette indicates how this is worked through in relation to the transference.

T: You were talking about some feelings you had toward your father. You are angry at him because he is not doing his job. He's not doing his job toward your mother, giving her emotional support, so you and your brother and other people feel compelled to take up that responsibility.

P: I wondered if you were going to be angry at me. You know, what are you doing walking down here with a girl? That's what I thought.

T: Why would I be angry at you?

P: (*Sigh*) I don't know. That I shouldn't be with a woman. I should do things that men do, you know. When I was a kid my father always said, "Play ball." You know, I wanted to go out with my girlfriend. My father would say, "Play basketball, play baseball." You know, go to the pool with him. Sports. All those activities.

T: So, you see, your father was inviting you to join him in those activities and you said, "No, no, I'm with a woman, with mother." See, there's a very powerful struggle between you and the authority figures, whereby you experience your father and me as forbidding you to have sexual intercourse with women. And you are going to defy that. To do everything you can to do the opposite. And then you experience that I am angry. You experience me as angry because you feel that you are engaging in a forbidden act, flirting with a woman (*P: laughs*) in this hospital who happens to work for me (*P: "Oooooh"*), and then you feel that I'm going to be angry.

P: Yeah. (*Laughs*) Could be. So why am I doing that?

T: You are challenging me.

P: Then it goes back to my fight with my father and my mother.

T: That seems to be the case. You always thought that your father was very stern and very angry, but you felt very guilty in relation to your father because you had all those wishes for your mother. You felt your father was saying, "You keep away from my woman and come with me and be a man like me." And you say, "No. Let me have those wishes for mother. Let me have this warm erotic relationship with her, and you, father, go and swim and play golf."

P: Jerk. (*Laugh*) He didn't know what he was missing. (*Laugh*)

T: So you see what you were afraid of was your own impulses, which you felt were going to get you in trouble.

P: Yes, sometimes I feel like I want to fuck every woman I see in the street. (*Mhm*) When I'm with Sarah we hang out for a while and then I always, you know, got to go to bed with her. I like it. It feels good.

After this session there is a decrease in his intense anxiety vis-à-vis the therapist, a reduction in his need to be distant from the therapist, and an increased capacity for constructive participation in the therapeutic process.

In addition, the patient begins to experience the therapist as a "real" person, and a process of identification starts.

P: Well, it was a new experience last week. You know, I kind of saw that you weren't my father, you weren't a lot of people. You're just a doctor, you're a person who's here. You were you, not anybody else.

Following this exchange, the patient feels much closer to the therapist as a man, to his father, to his brothers and even begins to fantasize about associating with construction workers of whom he was terrified in the past. A few sessions later the patient has gotten a job as a skilled carpenter on a construction site and discusses with the therapist, with evident pleasure, his capacity to participate in the playful, masculine activities of the group. As a corollary, his masochistic behavior toward women is diminished, and he is able to assert himself in a constructive way with his girlfriend.

Reference

Greenson, R. (1967). *The Technique and Practice of Psychoanalysis.* New York: International Universities Press.

Chapter 9

RESOLUTION

MANUEL TRUJILLO, M.D.
ARNOLD WINSTON, M.D.

The resolution and termination phases in short-term dynamic psychotherapy are both crucial to the successful outcome of the therapeutic process. They tend to unfold together in rapid sequence in patients who present with relatively uncomplicated oedipal psychopathology. In these patients, resolution and termination follow the uncovering and working-through phase often without transition.

Steps of the
Resolution Process

The main task of the resolution phase is the consolidation of the gains obtained in the earlier phases: there is typically a full acknowledgment of the oedipal wishes and a reformulation of the patients' real relationship to their parents. Frequently this involves a more genuine acceptance of the parents' positive and negative aspects and the emergence of previously hidden features such as intimacy and closeness, as well as areas of personal and professional identification.

The Emergence of Positive Feelings
Toward the Oedipal Rival: Sandra G.

The patient Sandra G. is a married woman in her midthirties who had suffered from three years of panic attacks. The early phase of treatment had brought into the foreground a frank oedipal dream where she sees herself. " . . . In the dream I'm having intercourse with my father and he whispers, 'Don't tell Mommy'."

The process of uncovering brings out the more deeply repressed negative feelings toward the patient's mother. These are first experienced toward her mother-in-law, whom she cared for during an episode of a terminal illness. In session 6, (Chapter 7) we saw how the patient becomes aware of her ambivalent feelings for her mother-in-law:

T: Do you know why you couldn't let yourself feel good?

P: I think it had to do with my mother-in-law. It would be hard to feel good while she was sick and dying.

T: Your thoughts—that she'd be better off dead—what part did they play in this?

P: I think I punished myself for those thoughts. Somehow if she didn't feel good and I didn't feel good, it was okay.

T: What were you punishing yourself for?

P: Wanting her dead and wanting everything all right for me, my marriage good, and a baby.

A few minutes later in the same interview:

T: Isn't there a parallel here with your feelings toward your mother? That it was hard to let yourself be angry with her?

P: Well with my mother-in-law it's all clearer; with my mother it's all more subconscious. I did have the fantasy that my mother would just go away, but I'd push it out of my mind. I didn't think it was right to have those thoughts, wishing she was out of the picture.

T: What were the fantasies about your mother going away?

P: Well, she had heart trouble—maybe—Grandma said

> she had a heart murmur — I still don't know to this day if there is anything wrong with her heart or not. I never wished her dead — never — in fact, sometimes I'd be afraid she'd die, if she had heart trouble. What I wished was that she would just go away.

T: Your wishes about her are very important for your understanding your own feelings. Could you remember any more about them?

P: Well, I'd think maybe she'll die, but I wouldn't take it all the way. I mean, I didn't wish she would die. In the fantasy she would just go away. Then most of the fantasy would be about me and Daddy. How I'd change the furniture. That he would be an adult with me. That I would listen to his problems at work — my mother never did — how I'd be important to him. I'm feeling very sad now, just thinking how hard it was to have a father — I had to fantasize to be close to him. That is sad.

This session brings into the focus the patient's repressed negative feelings toward her mother. They promote a train of events that include the acknowledgment of these negative and hostile feelings, a breakdown of the distance with which she typically relates to her mother, and a working through into the many, heretofore unexplored, sides of her relationship to her mother.

By the ninth treatment session (Chapter 8) she brings into the focus her competitive feelings toward her mother vis-a-vis doing housework.

> I don't like to do housework — it gets me angry. You know it connects to the past — my having to do the housework; my mother couldn't do it. I've always been better able to cope than my mother. In my mind I've been saying I am a better wife than you are, but I didn't feel comfortable about that.

As the psychotherapy proceeds, the patient links those past competitive feelings with the present, i.e., her fear of winning in tennis and her fear of performing and speaking in public. Then she shifts back to the core oedipal focus where she experiences her fear of "exhibiting myself in front of my father the way my mother did." Characteristically, the late working-through phase brings into play intense and deeply felt wishes and feelings in multiple areas of the patient's real and fantasy life. This patient can meaningfully experience her competitiveness and fear in her past relationship to mother vis-à-vis father in relationship to housework. Equally important is her experience of competitive, hostile, death wishes in her actual relationship with her mother-in-law, whose illness interferes with the patient's closeness to her husband.

The task of the resolution phase is to confirm, repeat, and consolidate these insights from many vantage points. Typically, the patients move with freedom between past and present feelings as they restructure their view of themselves and their objects from the new emerging perspective of their acknowledged negative wishes. This patient, Sandra G., in session 12 introduces for the first time a positive picture of her mother.

T: You said there must have been something positive about your mother.

P: Yes, in some ways she defended me with my father, who was very Victorian about clothing. I remember going shopping with her. She complimented me, encouraged me . . . in her own way there was encouragement. She was less punitive, for instance, about sin. She said, "don't worry." My father said, "That's a sin, you can't do it." Like looking at a magazine with nude people. He would become easily alarmed.

With patients who suffer from relatively uncomplicated psychopathology with little character involvement, the resolution phase increases the patient's mastery over impulses and feelings and enables the patient to acknowledge ambivalent impulses. Internal object images are reorganized accordingly. With patient Sandra G., once her competitive impulses are acknowledged, she can experience the positive aspects of her relationship with her mother, and her mother as a person, as well as feeling a genuine closeness to her mother. The patient can meaningfully experience guilt and remorse also frequently for the first time.*

Editor's note: As outlined in Chapter 2, the little girl needs to devalue the mother and make her bad (1) in the service of individuation and (2) in the service of the fantasy of being preferred by father. The picture of the mother changes with the

In this same session 12 the patient, after reviewing some positive moments in her relationship with her mother, is able, with little prodding from the therapist, to acknowledge the guilt feelings stemming from competitiveness with her mother, her intrusiveness, and her unconscious death wishes. Following this therapeutic sequence, the patient becomes remorseful and mournful of the lost relationship with her mother. During the session she becomes pensive and sad and states:

T: It seems as we talk, you become a little more aware of what your mother was able and not able to provide.

P: (*With sadness*) I fear I lost out in a lot of things — part of my childhood.

Following this experience, the patient indirectly introduces the issue of termination for the first time. With this type of patient, termination characteristically occurs without difficulty in one to three sessions. She starts with her feelings about leaving her job.

T: Was this the last weekend?

P: Yes, today is the last day. I am going back and giving my keys.

T: What's that been like? Leaving?

P: Well, it's been, it's been a lot of work. My girlfriend happened to have planned her vacation this week so I haven't been with her. It has been hard to say goodbye on some levels, and on other levels I noticed hostility. I think part of it is because I am leaving and they're angry too. Half of me says, "Good, I'm getting out of here," and half says "I feel a little sad." It's been a home feeling, a homey kind of atmosphere to a certain extent.

---

resolution of the Oedipus complex, and we often come to realize that the jealousy and hatred attributed to the oedipal mother is a projection of that which was felt by the little girl. Memory of the mother of the oedipally fixated woman is characteristically distorted in this fashion to a greater or lesser degree. The rejection of the mother by the child may set in motion a deteriorating relationship between them, as the mother responds to this rejection in a way that is determined by her own dynamics.

T: So you feel a little like you are leaving home. You are associating it with leaving your family.

P: Yah, then I realize I'm having a hard time leaving my family. I hope to be ready to leave. I want to leave. I haven't allowed myself really to feel sad. I feel sad but I haven't sat there and thought about it that much. I just came in very confused.

T: Came in . . .

P: Today, not knowing why I was feeling that way I . . .

T: I wonder if you are not also involved in ending treatment, feelings about that.

P: I've questioned how I'm going to feel, are my palpitations going to end, am I going to be able to work out things on my own? I feel like I am going to continue to grow more, make connections, but then there has been some question as to what exactly is the precise moment to do it.

To recapitulate, the resolution phase in patients suffering from psychopathology based on a relatively uncomplicated oedipal focus, and few, if any, character complications accomplishes the consolidation of the insight into the patient's core psychopathology. The tasks that the patient faces include the full acknowledgment of sexual and aggressive impulses, both mixed and ambivalent in relation to the objects of the patient's past. All the feelings should be experienced in relation both to the parent of the opposite sex and to the parent of the same sex. There may be other significant people (siblings, other relatives) who also figure prominently in the patient's earlier constellation, and they also have to be included in the working-through process. These patients readily experience the anxiety, sadness, and remorse associated with their hostile and sexual impulses and with their unconscious involvement in the life of their parents. With Sandra G. the sequential and systematic experiencing of her anger and competitiveness with her mother had a profoundly liberating effect and gave her considerable freedom to perceive and relate to her mother in a positive fashion. This freeing of new energies through the redirection of instinctual drives allows the patient to complete important developmental tasks.

Acceptance of tenuous identification becomes possible regarding the parent of the same sex and of the opposite sex. For the parent of the opposite sex the reduced need to idealize or disparage allows the patient a more realistic perception and acknowledgment of commonalities and desirable traits without threat to the sense of self-identity. With the parent of the same sex, closeness and intimacy can also foster a new process of identification that does not promote guilt.

The nature of the therapeutic work required at this level includes gentle effort in the direction of maintaining a therapeutic focus and of ensuring that all the dimensions of the oedipal feelings (i.e., positive and negative feelings, sexual and aggressive drives) are experienced toward both parents. Intense transference work is rarely needed unless there are pronounced negative shifts in the unconscious therapeutic alliance.

Complications: Loss Focus or Character Pathology

Complications of this phase may arise in those patients where there is a loss focus or substantial pregenital or character pathology. These patients easily develop a transference neurosis that cannot be worked through in the context of short-term therapy. It is essential that this type of patient be identified early enough in the evaluation process so that the complications can be avoided or contained. Other manifestations of the presence of some degree of pregenital and character pathology include early regressive swings and, rarely, depression and acting-out behavior. When these appear in patients who have been well selected, they are very responsive to transference interpretation.†

---

†*Editor's note*: Some patients may constitute a false positive group with respect to selection on the basis of competitive dynamics. They may appear to be oedipal, but in fact the triangle either relates (1) to the situation of a third person (father or sibling) as intruder into the maternal dyad, or (2) to the externalization and acting out of the split in the primary attachment object, with the idealized object image being transferred to the father while the bad and persecutory object image remains with the mother. The eroticized relationship with this primitive idealization of the father may be the basis for an intractable erotic transference with a persisting belief that the therapist reciprocates these feelings but is hiding them for profes-

Both systematic transference interpretation and some degree of confrontation of character defenses are required in patients who suffer from *moderate* degrees of character psychopathology in the context of oedipal problems.

The following set of vignettes describes the technical requirements of the resolution phase in a patient of this type.

Interpretation of Defensive Regression: Leo C.

This is a continuation of the case of Leo C. who is in his early fifties and who is being treated for free-floating and situational anxiety of four year's duration. His numerous prior attempts at psychotherapy ended prematurely. In addition to his oedipal psychopathology, the patient suffered from obsessional defenses such as intellectualization and isolation of affect. Mild to moderate masochistic traits complete the dynamic picture. Early treatment sessions brought to the forefront intense oedipal wishes for his mother and severe castration anxiety. There were early memories of a distant relationship with his father, whom he described as punitive and competitive, in particular for the mother's attention. Night terror and a fear of darkness were continually present during early childhood. Derivatives of castration anxiety appeared from the very first interview. He vividly remembers an occasion at the age of 13 when his parents locked his sister in a closet and her thumb got caught in the door. He has a strong memory of his sister's screams and her thumb, crushed and hanging when the door was opened.

The early phase of treatment developed quite uneventfully. The therapeutic process unfolds through the uncovering phase in an orderly manner. The focus is easily developed around a relatively un-

sional reasons. Kohut (1972) distinguishes the hysteric who looks like a narcissistic personality (and who might be suitable for brief psychotherapy) from the narcissistic personality who looks like an hysteric (and would *not* be suitable for brief psychotherapy). The importance of eliminating the more serious character disorder as a candidate for brief psychotherapy cannot be overemphasized. Trial interpretations during the evaluation process should clarify the situation. If the patient responds poorly to these interpretations, suitability is questionable. Instead of moving the patient forward, they will constitute a narcissistic injury.

complicated oedipal theme: there is castration anxiety manifested via the episode of the sister's thumb. There is also evidence of emotional and physical closeness to his mother as well as a frightened distance from his father, who is perceived exclusively as a rival.

The working-through phase requires systematic confrontation of character defenses, including massive denial of angry feelings and masochistic submission in interpersonal confrontations.

Sessions 15 to 16 represent a shift in the defensive pattern from chronic intellectualization toward a deeper acceptance and experience of negative feelings in the transference. The shift occurs following session 15 during which the therapist confronts the patient's denial of irritation with the therapist after the session had been repeatedly interrupted by phone calls related to an emergency. The patient is now able to contact his fears of retaliation at a deeper level: "Yes . . . the fear of being hurt is devastating . . . ."

With these more complicated patients the consolidation phase requires that therapeutic work be done at the emotional level. The shift from the cognitive-intellectual approach to the emotional sphere may necessitate vigilant attention on the part of the therapist and efforts to maintain the therapeutic focus as well as the openness to experiencing emotion.

The patient may use intellectual defenses, character defenses (passivity, masochism, submission), or regress into a power struggle based on issues of domination and control. All these maneuvers can typically be overcome by adherence to the therapeutic focus while actively interpreting any obstacles to maintain it. A very important technical ingredient at this stage involves the avoidance of issues unrelated to the therapeutic direction (side issues). The therapist should also avoid being bullied or scared into defensively based regressive swings.

With patient Leo C. in session 20 his own unconscious detects and stops a potentially regressive swing in the following dream:

> "I had this dream after last week's session. I'm embarrassed to tell you, but I think it's important. I was debating whether to wipe myself. There was a restaurant further back and out walked my boss dressed as a waiter. He said, 'You dropped something' and then picked up the toilet paper from the floor and gave it to me. This was not the big boss,

the one who is more like my father, but the more immediate one."

The patient catches himself, as it were, in the act of debating
whether or not to shift into a power-dominated dependency struggle with the therapist, but instead opts for autonomy.

Sometimes, even in well-evaluated patients the regression can
reach a higher level of intensity. Patients may even appear to be suffering from "pregenital," "oral," or "borderline" features that tend
to frighten the therapist into either inactivity or abandonment of
the neutral stance. The threat to these patients is termination, which
the patients unconsciously perceive as imminent once they sense the
therapeutic gains made in the working-through and resolution phases.
In this patient, in session 21, there is a recrudescence of symptoms
of anxiety. He says, "This is a critical period; for the first time in
16 years I really felt good. Then a few days ago I came back down
to reality and felt anxious again."

He is also plagued by fantasies and fears of death, especially
the death of his wife and son. This is handled by interpreting it in
the context of his fear of termination, and the patient goes on to
an uneventful termination with successful outcome at follow-up.

The unconscious fantasies of self-object destruction (including
destruction of the therapist as well as the need to masochistically
atone for death wishes) are reduced enough to account for the intrapsychic restructuring that is characteristic of the consolidation phase.
Again this patient's interpersonal relationships become more pristine
and genuine, with less interference of primitive aggressive sexual-
ization.

The patient found himself enjoying the company of peers for
the first time in his life. He gave a reception for a member of his
department and made a toast in his honor, which he had been unable to do before. He also describes several events that demonstrate
a great deal of warmth in his relationship with his father.

Summarizing, the resolution phase in short-term dynamic psychotherapy follows the stages of uncovering and working through
and adds depth and stability to the gains of the therapeutic work.
The insights acquired in the earlier phases are deepened and incorporated into the psychic apparatus. These changes typically occur
in an atmosphere of increasingly intense emotional experiencing.
There are also significant shifts in the patient's sense of himself and

in his relating to others. Frequently there is an increasing capacity to acknowledge and gratify impulses as well as to renounce certain wishes. In relation to the parent of the opposite sex, the patient is able to desexualize his drives. In its place, genuine affection becomes possible and forms the basis for a gratifying friendship. Similar changes occur in relation to the parent of the same sex; here the impulses to displace and defeat in competition give way to feelings of equality, mutuality, and altruistic relating. In real life the patient frequently experiences the pleasures of giving and receiving gifts. From these grounds there is a relaunching of the process of identification. Deeply held family, social, political, and religious values and aspirations become reexamined and valued.

The task of the therapist at this phase includes the maintenance of therapeutic foci as well as the prevention of the development of the transference neurosis by active interpretation. The emotional concomitants of insight should be maintained by alert recognition of excessively intellectualized dry spells. In patients suffering from complicated multifocal psychopathology, one might see at this phase a regression into power struggles or such states as helplessness, anxiety, or a recrudescence of symptoms. They frequently subside by adherence to the focus, maintenance of neutrality, active interpretation of the nuclear conflict, and some transference work. The confidence of the therapist who works in the face of apparently regressive swings rests in his intimate knowledge of the patient's psychopathology acquired in the evaluation phase. The therapist needs to ensure that all facets and dimensions of the patient's core psychopathology will appear in the therapeutic focus, since completeness of the therapeutic work seems to correlate with outcome and stability of results. This completeness of the work requires that both positive (libidinal) and negative (aggressive) feelings are worked through in relationship to both father and mother. Excessive focusing on one of these dimensions may promote therapeutic misalliance and detract from a positive outcome or lead into a transference neurosis.*

---

*Long-term psychotherapy often both enables and reinforces defensive regression which, if not confronted and interpreted, may set in motion an intractable resistance. The process of therapy itself may become subsumed within the defense. The firm time limit of brief psychotherapy confronts both therapist and patient with the necessity of dealing with the issue promptly and consistently.

Reference

Kohut, H. (1972). Thoughts on narcissism and narcissistic rage. *Psychoanalytic Study of the Child* 72: 360–400.

Chapter 10

TERMINATION

MANUEL TRUJILLO, M.D.
ARNOLD WINSTON, M.D.

The problem of termination in psychotherapy and psychoanalysis has been given detailed theoretical examination in the psychoanalytic literature. Beginning with Freud's (1937) "Analysis Terminable and Interminable," much work has been accomplished by individual investigators as well as by special workshops and symposia of the American Psychoanalytic Association. There is, however, scant empirical evidence as to the role of termination in any kind of psychoanalytically based psychotherapy. Mann's (1973) theoretical approach to brief psychotherapy tends to bring into the psychotherapeutic focus conscious and unconscious universal experiences and conflicts relating to termination by the technical construct of rigidly defining the exact number of sessions. Issues such as polarities of dependence versus independence, activity versus passivity, adequate versus low self-esteem are easily mobilized by a preset termination phase. In Mann's own words, "Knowing the termination date at the start increases anxiety in respect to loss, as well as defenses against loss. The termination date is quickly repressed and the intensification of the defenses against separation and/or loss serves to highlight much of the nature of the present central issue and the means employed to master it."

Malan's (1963, 1976) two studies of psychotherapy are among the few sources of empirically validated psychotherapy hypotheses.

In his first study, which involved a variety of patients suitable for psychotherapy, Malan demonstrated that those therapies tended to be successful in which:

1. Transference arose early;
2. Negative transference was thoroughly interpreted;
3. The link was made between transference and the relation to the parents;
4. The patient was able to work through grief and anger about termination.

In addition, patients with whom the transference had been thoroughly interpreted tended to accept termination. Malan accepted for treatment patients suffering from a variety of disorders with diverse degrees of severity so that the findings apply to all patients without distinction. Sifneos' experience, as well as the findings of our own project, tends to indicate that for carefully selected patients with primarily oedipal focus psychopathology, termination occurs without problems. Frequently, the patient brings the issue out himself, often following a discussion of tangible changes in the patient's life. These changes relate to the working-through phase and are connected with therapeutic work at the nuclear conflict level. This tends to be a period of very active work; the patients gain emotional insight about significant areas of their lives. They also experience shifts in intrapsychic representations as well as changes in the perception of parents and other meaningful real objects. Typically, after recounting experiences of this type in a given session, the patient, either directly or indirectly, brings up the issue of termination.

Case Study: Sandra G.

For Sandra G., who had suffered from relatively uncomplicated oedipal psychopathology, the treatment process moved uneventfully from evaluation, to uncovering, and into the working-through phases. After a series of emotionally charged sessions, culminating in the patient's confrontation of her intense competitive feelings with her mother and her fear of punishment (see pp. 143–147, Chapter 8), the patient herself brings up the idea of termination, first indirectly through associations regarding a forthcoming job change. Shortly thereafter the sadness at a farewell party brings the issue up directly:

P: I guess I was able to face saying goodbye to all these people . . . Some I'll miss, some not so much (*Smiles*) . . . This is another way of growing up . . . and I wasn't particularly frightened . . . Well, I had some butterflies in my stomach but no palpitations . . . Not really. I have palpitations though, when I think about terminating therapy . . . Not palpitations, more the thought of what I am going to do if they recur . . .

T: What do you have in mind?

P: Well, I think I can fight on myself, live with it, and move ahead, rather than backward . . . I think I can take care of myself now . . . It's sad, but it's also true . . . nothing is perfect . . . it's a matter of what is enough. I guess this applies to my therapy too . . . can I let it end.

Typical of these patients, Sandra G. goes on working up to the last minute with very little prodding from the therapist. Meaningful issues are brought into the focus and dealt with in an atmosphere of real emotional interaction and deep involvement with their own affective process. It is as if a powerful process has been set in motion, which in the absence of severe character pathology, proceeds uninterrupted toward termination. At the end, the patient leaves the treatment without excessive difficulty, in an atmosphere of genuine gratitude. Frequently the patient (or patient and therapist jointly) recapitulate the dynamic and behavioral changes that have occurred throughout the therapy, but more intensely during the working-through phase.

In patients with more complicated psychopathology, but still within the oedipal spectrum, termination may bring about a transitory recrudescence of symptoms. This phenomenon, which according to Firestein (1968) is almost a universal aspect of the closing treatment phase in classical psychoanalysis in all patients, occurs only in certain patients in short-term dynamic psychotherapy. In these patients, specific symptoms (anxiety and depression) and defenses about termination have to be worked through.

Case Study: Leo C.

Leo C, the middle-aged man who came into treatment for anxiety attributed to problems at work completes his treatment in 23 sessions. In session 20 the patient discusses at length some changes that have occurred in his life and that he deems meaningful. He has been able, for the first time, to address a meeting of executives in his firm. The therapist then indicates, "You have made a great deal of progress. Do you think we should think about terminating treatment?" The patient responds with considerable anxiety, "I am concerned about the future . . . Can I continue to do well? If problems come up will I be able to solve them?" The patient goes on to discuss his fear of getting worse if a new problem should arise. The next session brings further discussion about a recurrence of symptoms and a mild regressive swing, indicated by fears of death. After this is actively interpreted in relation to the transference, the patient resumes the work of separation. Links are made between his passivity and fear of facing termination of treatment and his passivity in the past vis-à-vis his father, where it had the function of masking strong competitive feelings:

T: We know that you were passive with your father, afraid of him, yet you had a lot of strong feelings toward him.

P: Yes, I was afraid when he would push me, but I was angry with him too. Recently we were visiting with my parents, and he suggested we enter a duplicate bridge tournament. Actually a few years ago we played duplicate bridge together. That's when my anxiety started . . . I just couldn't do it.

Thus successful termination is linked in this patient's mind to intense competitiveness in his early relationship with his father.

T: So you will not "perform" here with me, as you wouldn't "perform" with your father.

P: This is self-defeating, like with my boss . . . If he asks me for a response I feel compelled to say no.

T: Yes, the feeling is to say no.

P: Yes, I get angry and become negative. I've let these feelings hold me back and stop me from doing what I
should be doing.

This work, at the level of transference, i.e., the interpretation
of the transferential meaning and implications of successful termination and his need to hold back from it, allows the patient to move
back into the focus and complete the psychotherapeutic work by
session 23.

In patients who, in addition to substantial and clearly identifiable oedipal psychopathology, also suffer from a significant loss,
the issue of termination is of paramount importance and requires
specific focused attention and techniques for its successful resolution. The following example illustrates the issues involved.

Case Study: Larry G.

The patient is a 30-year-old, single, unemployed man who entered
treatment because of an episode of depression related to his impending loss of a relationship with his girlfriend with whom he had established a passive, dependent, and unfulfilling relationship (see
pp. 151–156, Chapter 8).

This patient's oedipal psychopathology had been additionally
complicated by family dynamics such as an absent and distant father
and the seductive-dependent character structure of his mother, who
was emotionally very needy and dependent on the patient. These
family forces, in turn, intensified the patient's castration anxiety,
necessitating the adoption of homosexuality, passivity, and dependence as regressive defenses. Thus dependence and fear of loss became a second, relatively independent focus of this patient's psychopathology.

In the course of treatment this had appeared as fear of abandonment, linked with the therapist's scheduled two-week vacation.
The issue had to be worked through first as an issue of separation
and then had to be linked to its oedipal roots before the therapeutic

process could advance. The following are vignettes from session 4, before, and session 5, after the vacation took place.*

SESSION 4

The patient started the session with visible anxiety and dejection, talking about feeling "terrible . . . lonely . . . depressed," for reasons that he cannot pinpoint. He says that nothing works in his life and that he always winds up on the losing end. He talks about Judy, a former girlfriend who, after having abused him, suddenly dropped him.

P: She waved the flag of the relationship all the time . . . the relationship, the relationship, you know, it has to continue. So I felt I sacrificed a lot of progress, a lot of growth for the sake of that relationship, that was just a piece of shit . . . The last couple of months were hell!!

T: You see, there is a whole area here, relating to feelings of loss and abandonment. Now we know that it's in relation to women, and it's in relation to men too, like, for example, in relation to your father. How about here with me?

P: I feel panicky that you're going away . . . I feel scared that you're going away.

T: Yes. In the last two weeks your girlfriend has left and I am leaving . . .

P: (*Sigh*) (*Long pause*) I don't know how I'm going to deal with it.

Editor's note: As mentioned earlier, the steps in the resolution of the Oedipus complex, and thus of the phases of treatment, do not necessarily take place in a linear manner. We will see manifestations of working through in the predominantly uncovering phase. In a parallel fashion, termination issues will overlap with the predominantly working-through phase of treatment, especially when there are significant abandonment or loss issues. The therapist must maintain the flexibility to make these shifts as long as they are kept within the focus. Dealing with these issues promptly lays the groundwork for actual termination and protects the contract for brief treatment.

T: What thoughts do you have about my leaving?

P: I've been in different kinds of therapy and like this therapy I've never gone back like here we are going back . . . I'm talking about when I'm 3 years old and 5 years old . . . I'm searching for things . . I'm not going to have anybody to talk to and I'm not going to be able to deal with things myself. I'm going to be really scared. I'm feeling now like I felt yesterday morning (*crying*). I started thinking about coming home after school and nobody at home. It was going to be a dark, empty, quiet house . . . And there would be absolutely nothing but me and my thoughts, and my thoughts are going to scare me.

T: What about those thoughts? What about those thoughts is going to scare you?

P: These feelings I have. Feeling left, feeling abandoned . . . Like with my parents when I was a kid, they went out one night and left me with my little sister. I didn't think they were coming back . . . and they used to fight and talk about divorce and I would wonder what it is like if they get a divorce.

T: What would it be like if they got a divorce?

P: What is it like to live without a . . . without a father?

T: Did you think about that? You must have a lot of feelings, you and your mother together and he out of the picture.

P: That terrifies me.

T: So does the idea of my leaving . . . because in a way the hope is that if I disappear you will hold onto your relationship with Susan.

P: I'm afraid that if you go it's back to square one . . . I like it but also I'm back to a helpless little boy.

The session following the therapist's vacation also starts on a regressive note. The patient says that he feels like an "emotional cripple." Yet, paradoxically, he looks better and sounds more articulate and better integrated. As the session proceeds, we are able to see that his feeling like a cripple was linked to the therapist's vacation.

T: What other thoughts have you had about me in the last two weeks?

P: I wondered what you were doing. If you were on vacation or if you were in the city. I wondered where you went on your vacation or if you just hung out at home, or even if you were on vacation.

T: Could you develop those thoughts?

P: I thought maybe you weren't on vacation; maybe you just took some time off, a couple of days here and there and that you didn't want to do therapy with me.

T: Why would that be the case?

P: (*Sigh*) Because it's probably more exciting to do therapy with other people. More interesting, more stimulating to you. You make progress with other people. You just like other patients better than me.

This sequence of transference-based regression with a theme of separation, loss, and abandonment reappears with great intensity toward the end of therapy. Until session 10 there had been a number of hours of intensive therapeutic work. The uncovering and working-through process had proceeded without regressive swings. The patient acquired cognitive and emotional insight in many areas of his core conflict. He clearly experienced his intense fear of his father, which is associated with his early erotic feelings for his mother. The same feelings have been experienced vis-a-vis his older brother and in the transference, where he clearly sees himself in competition with the therapist. In the course of the therapy he developed clearly identifiable erotic feelings for a number of women who were linked to the therapist. He became flirtatious with secretaries, receptionists, and other females who worked near the therapist's office. As these feelings increased, his fear of castration also became evident via multiple derivatives (i.e., for awhile he had the compulsive need to go to the bathroom before each session because of intolerable tension in his penis.)

By this time (session 10) there were clear changes in some of the patterns of behavior that had initially brought him into therapy. He felt emotionally closer to his father and to the therapist, whom he could experience both as a person and as a man without the need for emotional distance and without the development of anxiety. He also became more assertive in his relationship with his girlfriend. He developed pride in his capacity to be self-reliant and work with his own hands, as well as in his capacity to take a stronger stand with his peers.

Some of these changes have been noticeable to people in his environment. His mother remarked that there is a different feel about him.

> P: She said, "I notice a big change in the last couple of months." I said, "I feel down and I get depressed." She said, "I know that, but you're functioning in a different way. You aren't bringing people down. You're not saying to everybody that you are such garbage that people better stay away from you. You're now depressed but in a different way."

As the patient saw these changes, he experienced intense anxiety and sadness. All of a sudden he became fearful that the therapist was going to "throw him out of the therapy." His response was a panic-ridden regression to his prior defense stance of "being a cripple." The patient wondered whether the therapist would refer him to group therapy so that he could learn to relate to people. The following dialogue ensues:

> P: Yeah, she's (*girlfriend*) kind of shut the door in. I might be able to stop relating to her in that one way (*as a cripple*) and do it in a different way.
>
> T: It is difficult.
>
> P: But she's cut me off.
>
> T: It is possible but difficult.
>
> P: She's cut me off. There's no room for possibility there.
>
> T: Then you also have to accept the fact that in your mind mother belongs to father and you are left to find your own person. All of this is painful, but I think that you have the resources to begin to put this in the framework of normality rather than in the framework of being a cripple. Perhaps your request has something to do with the fact that the thought has come to your mind that this therapy has to end someday.
>
> P: I wondered a lot about that today.

   т: When did you start to wonder.?

   p: Well, in the last couple of months, particularly in the
      last month.

   т: Is it possible that your sadness and depression have
      something to do with your seeing that you are going to
      lose this therapy and me as a person to relate to?

   p: I find it useful and it is helpful to me. If I were to ter-
      minate it in a week or two I don't know if I would be
      able to maintain myself and to develop any further. I'm
      scared too.

   т: That is why you are saying that you need more therapy,
      but actually I think that you can use your own resources
      to develop and grow. It is your fear that this psycho-
      therapy is coming to an end that has stirred up so much
      anxiety.

   In session 15 the patient again goes through an intensive struggle, but the therapy is terminated by mutual agreement, with the
patient having a strong sense that he can progress on his own. One-
and two-year follow-up indicated that there were significant symptomatic and dynamic changes that were maintained.

   To recapitulate, just as in classical psychoanalysis and psychoanalytically based open-ended psychotherapies, the termination process is a dynamic, vital part of the therapeutic process of short-term
dynamic psychotherapy. The patients enter and leave these processes
in different ways, depending on their defenses. Patients suffering
from uncomplicated oedipal psychopathology have no difficulty
entering this stage and require very little specialized therapeutic effort to accomplish termination. Where there is a loss or complicated
multifocal psychopathology, patients will require special attention
to separation issues. Successful working through of this problem
requires detailed attention to transferential implications.

References

Firestein, S. (1968). Problems of termination in the analysis of
   adults. Presented at the Annual Meeting of the American Psychoanalytic Association, Boston.

Freud, S. (1937). Analysis terminable and interminable. *Standard Edition* 23:216–253. London: Hogarth.

Malan, D. (1963). *A Study of Brief Psychotherapy*. New York: Plenum Press.

———(1976). *The Frontier of Brief Psychotherapy*. New York: Plenum Press.

Mann, J. (1973). *Time-Limited Psychotherapy*. Cambridge: Harvard University Press.

Chapter 11

CONFRONTATION OF CHARACTER DEFENSES: A CASE STUDY

ALTHEA J. HORNER, Ph.D.

The following material is from the brief treatment of a 40-year-old man who was employed in a highly responsible technical position in the communications industry in upstate New York. The presenting problem was his failure to advance in his work. A previous course of treatment with another therapist left the major transference resistance untouched, i.e., his passivity and failure to challenge the authority of the therapist.

Born and raised in upstate New York, his newly arrived Japanese family had reestablished a clan-style of life, with the extended family living within a single household in which the oldest uncle was the undisputed leader of the family. The patient was the middle of three children.

It should be noted that in the evaluation interview, the patient reported an inability to recall the early relationships with his parents, and he denied a significant emotional relationship in the present. Only one side of the triangle (the father side) was evident, and there only in terms of derivatives. Because he fit the diagnostic criteria and because he was highly motivated and interested in the brief approach, a decision was made to go ahead. The focus was defined as his fear of competing, of challenging authority, and of doing what he had to do to get ahead in his career.

What is interesting in this case is the emergence of the oedipal issues and his readiness to look at them in the context of the initially agreed-upon focus. Although this is an atypical case, adherence to the principles of brief treatment led to a breaking through of the character resistances so that the early repressed material could emerge. The oedipal situation itself was atypical as it involved the uncle, although the mother-father-patient triangle also soon became evident. The wish to admire the father and to be special to him was as strong as the wish to be special to the mother. The uncle interfered on both counts, while mother passively came between the children and their father.

The sessions reported here are predominantly from the uncovering phase of treatment, although in the 17th session we begin to see a shift to the working-through phase. It was only after a steady confrontation of character defenses that the underlying oedipal issues began to emerge. Although the therapist was a woman, the transference was characterized by his attitude toward the male authority figure, an amalgam of the feared uncle and the loved father.

Note especially the fast pacing and activity level of the therapist. This stands in sharp contrast to that of long-term treatment in which the therapist does not want to interfere with the associational process.

Session 1

P: I've watched my colleagues pass me by. I'm pushed around by circumstances and by others. I don't like that either. I'm afraid to speak up and tell how I feel, and then I make excuses to myself. I don't show leadership to my kids either. My wife is in control by default. We get along well, but there is a leadership problem. I stay in the background, but would like to set an example to my kids. At work I have a reputation for being a good worker, but I'm not the one to be in charge. Now I'm in a situation where I have to interact more and have to tell others what to do.

T: How is that for you?
(Inquiry aimed at moving away from intellectualization to experience.)

P: I feel defensive. I'm not used to telling people what to do. I don't feel superior to them, so I'm apologetic. I try to cover all grounds so I won't be attacked or criticized.

T: How does that work for you?
(*Move to making the defenses less syntonic.*)

P: I get cooperation. I bring the other side in so they're in it with me, so it's as much my problem as theirs. We're on equal footing. They accept my comments.

T: It sounds like it works but you don't feel good about it.

P: We all want the same goal, but I don't like the feeling I have inside. People who were junior pass over me. Since I saw Dr. L, I realized the situation more. My unfortunate old habits are strong and I fall back. I don't retreat to a shell as much, but if I'm not on guard I fall back.

T: What was the impact of Dr. L's death for you?
(*Exploring unresolved transference with previous therapist. The patient had not been in treatment for some time when Dr. L. died suddenly and unexpectedly.*)

P: It was a big loss. I was sad. I thought he was selfish. He could have helped me and others.

T: You sound angry.
(*Clarifying affect: tone of voice and posture.*)

P: I'm disappointed. I recalled I liked him. I could communicate very well with him. It was a sudden loss, a disappointment.

T: And what was the effect of the disappointment on you?

P: I don't recall feeling any different. I saw him once a month. Before that it was every week. After a year it didn't have to be as frequent. I went back to recharge my batteries. It was the holiday season so I didn't see him that time. I felt sad and disappointed, but no other feeling.

T: You saw him as an energy source.
(*The dynamic of the unresolved transference.*)

P: I relied on him. It could be an area I was so used to as a kid. My parents took care of everything. I was protected and sheltered. That's where I get my attitude of dependency. It's more comfortable to have someone to depend on. That all came out with analyzing. I'm aware that I'm emotionally and psychologically dependent.

T: It sounds like the wish for someone strong to rely on is part of the overall pattern.
(*Exploring motivation.*)

P: That's an area he and I covered.

T: Was that your insight?
(*Transference issue.*)

P: There were two levels of understanding. The intellectual level was very reasonable. But the emotional level had no experience or exposure, so I don't know. I can rationalize or justify. I'm not used to the gut level. If I have a gut level response, I will be passive. I take the path of least resistance. I try to please. I'm not sure of myself.

T: You had a reaction when I said I would not see you for what Dr. L. charged you and said my fee would be higher. What were those feelings?
(*Responding to transference allusion of previous statement.*)

P: I came prepared intellectually.

T: What do you mean?
(*Asking for clarification.*)

P: I'm embarrassed. I have no strong feelings.

T: You're embarrassed suggests you turn your negative feelings onto yourself.
(*Exploring defensive style.*)

P: That would be consistent with my behavior. At work and in general, when I make an assertion and someone doubts or questions me, I first react as though I did something wrong rather than say he doesn't know.

T: Can you give me an example?
(*Asking for specifics.*)

P: With my boss, Ted. I'd have an idea about a problem and say the way I see the priorities are. Then he'd come back and say the other way is better. Then I'd withdraw.

T: How did you feel toward Ted at that moment?
(*Probe for feelings versus obsessive style.*)

P: As we are talking I am experiencing fear. Maybe I'm not being too accurate. When Ted comes back with a rebuttal, the only reaction I remember is annoyance. I don't know if there was fear then. Then I felt resignation — a "you're the boss" attitude.

T: You experienced fear as you told me about it.

P: On coming here, I felt it in my gut, like the first time with Dr. L. It gradually disappeared. The thought just occurred to me, when I first meet someone, I'm on guard. Then I get used to the situation. I bring it up because it relates to my dealing with my inner self. When I first met Dr. L., I tried to get to my inner feelings. But I drift back to my old self. Also with my boss. When I'm in a more assertive mood, I'd go in and interact with Ted in a different way and would get more favorable results, especially in the first few instances. But I'd drift back.

T: You said before that you resent him, then you withdraw, and then turn the negative feelings on yourself. Let's look at what starts the drift back.
(*Exploring defensive style, which will be evident in resistance.*)

P: I set a goal, like a pay raise. I prepare myself intellectually and justify it. Then I talk to Ted. Once it's done, it doesn't matter if the goal is accomplished or not. I relax. There's nothing to work on.

T: It's hard to hold on to your ambition.
(*Clarifying motivation.*)

P: To my goal.

T: You said you want to move ahead.

P: True. It did occur to me that if I set specific goals I'd do better. That's curing the symptom. I could set ten goals.

T: You're talking about justifying a single act, as contrasted with dealing with your ambition and your aggression
in general.
(*Cutting through denial of aggression.*)

P: Maybe that *is* the problem. I tend to drift back because
I don't have what it takes to own my ambition and aggression.

T: It goes underground.
(*Interpretation of defense.*)

P: I'm not sure what my ambitions are. Maybe to be at
the limit of my potential. That's easier said than done.

T: Something stands in the way.

P: Yes, but I don't know what.

T: Our time is almost up. What are your feelings about
our session and about continuing?

P: You're very sharp.

T: How do you feel about that?

P: It's very exciting and interesting, the things you put out.
I have a picture in my mind that Dr. L. and I painted
together of my background. You pinpoint my ambition.
I'm not at ease with it.

T: What are your feelings?

P: It could be beneficial. I don't think I can come every
week.
(*He avoids answering, but time is up.*)

T: If we are to work in the brief format it will have to be
every week, and it will be limited to 40 sessions in all.
(*Reestablishing the contract.*)

P: After the 40 weeks, would I be able to come back peri-
odically as I did with Dr. L.?

T: No. Our job will be to figure out why it was necessary
for you to do that. You said it was to recharge your
batteries. That implies you continued to see him as the
source of power. That's what we'll have to understand.
(*The therapist clarifies the contract and the focus.*)

Session 2

T: What was your reaction to our last session?

P: I appreciated it intellectually. It made me think. I'm aware I don't do my best. I'm too tired much of the time and don't want to be bothered.

T: You said it was fear and resentment with Ted. (*Cutting through the denial.*)

P: That's correct. Maybe fear of rejection.

T: How does that feel?

P: It felt bad.

T: How do you feel toward the person who rejects you?

P: Resentment. I feel bad about myself and blame myself.

T: You turn the resentment anger onto yourself. But first you felt it toward Ted.

P: It might be meaningful if I cast it in another light. I was rejected by my parents and there was nothing I could do.
(*Obsessive helplessness.*)

T: Give me an example.

P: It was a pattern, the way I was brought up. If I was obedient and got good grades, I'd get a pat on the back. If I did anything out of line, like fight, they'd come down on me.

T: And do what?

P: It's a general impression.

T: You are staying away from a specific memory. (*Confronting the resistance.*)

P: I don't remember my childhood.

T: Did they beat you?

P: They'd scold me.

T: What did they say?

P: That I shouldn't do that, that so and so was better behaved.

T: Like who?

P: My cousins. It was a big family, and we all lived in the same house.

T: Which cousins?

P: I don't remember. They'd say the other kids are better.

T: How did that make you feel?

P: I may be making it up.

T: What are you experiencing right now?

P: Fear. It's overwhelming.
   (*This should have been explored in terms of the transference.*)

T: Did they threaten you with punishment?

P: No. They'd say if you behave badly, you make us look bad to the other relatives. That was the theme.

T: And there is fear in that?

P: Yes. I'm not sure if I loved my parents. I respected them. I didn't want them to look bad.

T: How does that work with other authority figures — not making them look bad? How does it work with Dr. L. and with Ted and with me?

P: I don't do anything. That's just a premise I work on.

T: What do you do to make Ted look bad?

P: It never occurs to me that what I do will make him look bad or good. I don't want to look bad in his eyes.

T: If you were smarter and knew better what to do, that would make him look bad to others.
   (*Moving toward the conflict.*)

P: I don't want to tell people what to do. It means I look better than they are. It didn't occur to me in relation to Ted consciously.

T: To succeed you have to be better. You say that's a bad thing to do to someone.

P: It makes sense. I've been feeling fear for the last ten minutes.

T: Is it because of what I said?

P: Yes. This whole conversation makes me afraid.

T: What are your associations to it?

P: It rubs off to my boy. He's 10 and a top student. My wife and I can't stand that he tries to be no different from the other kids. There's peer pressure. He purposely avoids standing out.

T: Like you.

P: Yes.

T: How do you feel toward your son for doing that?

P: I was mad. He is better. He doesn't have to hide it.

T: You want him to look better and make you look good.

P: I want him to feel good about himself. I don't expect any benefit from it.

T: So then why are you *mad* at him.
(*Cutting through the denial.*)

P: He had a chance to play the piano for our friends. I wanted him to play. He made excuses. He could show how good he is.

T: You're angry, not worried.
(*Clarifying affect: nonverbal behavior.*)

P: Maybe the fact that if he performed I'd look good.

T: And you're angry that he didn't.

P: That makes sense.

T: You're wanting to look good sounds like it was a competitive situation.

P: I'm mad at myself about it.
(*Therapist should have noted he turned anger on himself here.*)

T: There is a conflict if to look good makes someone else look bad.

P: That's not true. There are occasions I feel good about explaining things to others. This week there was a problem to be solved. I explained the solution and felt good.

I was in control. That only happens when I have all the information. If I'm missing a piece I don't have the guts to come out and say what I think. I qualify what I say. It's okay if the other doesn't know anything or if I know everything.

T: Where you are clearly superior.

P: Where I have the upper hand and there are no questions. When someone asks a question and I try to explain, I withdraw and crumble before I have time to think out an answer. I'm defensive though I know the answer.

T: Can you give me a specific example?

P: With Ted. Also the boss. Bosses reinforce the fear. Colleagues too, but not as much.

T: Like who?

P: Jack. He's more knowledgeable. I divide them into people I'm defensive with. The other group is easy-going, but I'm also defensive with them. But I do better.

T: It depends on how much power the other person has.

P: Yes. Or they know more.

T: How do you feel toward someone who knows more?

P: Respect. If it's someone I've known for some time, I don't mind asking them a simple question. If I barely know them, I shy away, though I need the answer. The way I feel when I talk to someone who is more knowledgeable—the word is subversive? Is that the word?

T: You're also thinking the word subservient?

P: Yes.

T: Do you know what subversive means?

P: Not lackey. Not challenging what they say. A "yes" man.

T: Subversive?

P: Spies. I mean subservient. There are two groups.

T: With one you enjoy being powerful and with the other you are subservient.

P: Yes. I enjoy being powerful.

T: So when someone is powerful over you, they have what you want. How does that make you feel?

P: I don't know.

T: Do you like them?
(*Pushing through the denial.*)

P: Not in particular. Ted. I don't care for him. Or Len.

T: What do you dislike about Len?

P: He's a stronger case. He manipulates people. He uses people to serve his own qualifications.

T: So how do you feel toward him?

P: I don't like him.

T: Does he make you angry?

P: No. I don't like that word. When I'm with him I'm subservient.

T: The same process as with your parents?

P: I'm going to see why I'm mad at my kid in the same vein. Maybe I fool myself. I thought I was just worried about him.

T: Maybe it's both.
(*Stating the ambivalence.*)

P: Ted doesn't do the job of a manager. He isn't organized. It's harder to work for him.

T: And it's hard to challenge that.

P: There's nothing specific to challenge. He's even vaguer than I am. Len is a different bag.

T: You dislike him even more.

P: Definitely.

T: You said you were feeling fear when you first came in. Are you still?

P: Not as much. No matter how unpleasant a person may be, when I get to know them, I think I can get used to them.
(*Transference allusion.*)

T: And has that happened with me?

P: (*Laughing*) Maybe.

T: You experience me as unpleasant.

P: Yes. Last time I did. (*Laughs*) (*On the way out the door.*) How do you feel about me? That you detected hostility in me?

T: Let's talk about it next time.

Session 3

P: I'm uncomfortable talking to you. Usually I don't like people who come on strong. That's why I don't like Len. He's high-handed.

T: What do you do with that kind of person?

P: I don't like them. I don't do anything. If I disagree with him, if he makes a general comment of no consequence, I would ignore it. If it's something to do with my work, I'd be intimidated. I would go along with it.

T: If the person has more power than you, you're afraid to challenge him.

P: Yes. Also with Ted. Just because he's the boss, I withdraw. I don't even think clearly.

T: We've talked about how, in your background, to make the other look bad is a hostile thing to do.

P: Yes, it is.

T: Are you just being agreeable with me now?

P: We laid the framework last week. It makes sense.

T: With me as with Len, are you just being agreeable?

P: I don't like how things are. It's the way I behave, the way I react. Our relationship is different from me and Ted. Here it's different. I explore. I tend to challenge more.
   (*There is a good working alliance.*)

T: Last time on the way out you were concerned about my

reaction to detecting your hostility.
(*Reminding him of the negative transference.*)

P: I was only looking at myself. I don't like people who come on strong. A thought occurred to me. It might be my anticipation that you would come on strong and I prepared myself with hostility to protect myself. Maybe it's just your style.

T: Are you saying you're afraid of retaliation?

P: Intellectually I acknowledge that.

T: You wanted me to reassure you I wasn't mad.

P: Maybe. It's my behavior pattern, like my reaction to my parents.

T: There's a link between your aggression, power, and looking good.
(*Clarifying dynamics.*)

P: It's frustrating. I have the opportunity to advance, but I dare not. I'm afraid I'll fall on my face. There's fear in me. If I go too far out on a limb, someone might cut it.

T: Who is the somebody?

P: A colleague. People who are jealous.

T: A jealous colleague.

P: They would challenge my work.

T: What about your jealousy?

P: I don't like it.

T: How do you feel to those who are over you?

P: I don't like to be subservient at work. If it's someone in authority to me, I can't handle it.

T: Was there a specific situation this week?
(*Cut through generalizations.*)

P: Someone equal to Ted's boss asked me to look into a problem. Instead of feeling delight, a challenge, I was scared. I didn't show it. I thought how can I make myself look good in his eyes rather than about doing the job.

T: Does this put you in competition with Ted?

P: No, but he goes on to a different project. If I'm aggressive and forceful enough I can take over his responsibilities . . . advancement. But I'm too scared. I don't want to. Edgar came to me to ask me some advice. He normally goes to Ted. I was more afraid rather than accepting a challenge.

T: What would happen if you were to succeed?

P: It would feel good.

T: Then what could the feeling scared be about?

P: What if I don't do a perfect job. I won't look good. I would be shamed in front of my colleagues. I don't want that. A new woman has joined us. I've been in the department longer. She's the aggressive type and is taking more responsibility from Ted. I'm feeling left out.

T: You're in direct competition with her?

P: Yes, to compete for Ted's attention.
   (*A triangle.*)

T: How about for his job?
   (*Should have stayed with the triangle and the competition he was acknowledging with inquiry about the parental triangle.*)

P: I never thought about that.

T: Would you like his job?

P: I don't know.

T: But you said you liked being in the powerful position.

P: I like having the knowledge.

T: But power is a core issue, as compared with being subservient.

P: If I know there is power.

T: Knowledge is just the vehicle to power. You are reacting to this woman moving into your territory.

P: We have our own territory. Our work is not in conflict. At one time it was and I didn't like it.
   (*Denial of present conflict.*)

T: What were the circumstances?

P: I was responsible for the overall checking out the system. I'm the analyst. She's responsible for testing out the system. I didn't like working on it with her and thought I'd have to show that. I did it by being uncooperative.

T: You expressed your aggression passively.

P: Yes. Maybe she detected it. She probably talked to Ted and got herself off the project. I was in charge.

T: How did you feel about the situation?

P: Angry.

T: At whom?

P: Probably her.

T: How about the one who assigned her, who chose her over you?
   (*Looking for the triangle issues.*)

P: If I was angry at Ted it wasn't obvious.

T: You don't let yourself know who you are angry at. That is one defense you use.
   (*Confronting resistance.*)

P: Yes. I use the technique of not knowing.

T: You use being ignorant as an aggressive act.

P: I do that a lot.

T: You also avoid conflict by being aggressive in passive ways.

P: That's correct.

T: How do you feel about that?

P: I don't know. It worked.

T: What do you mean?

P: She backed off.

T: Did you feel you had won?

P: No.

T: You avoided the issue and don't feel good about yourself.

P: Yes. I did avoid it. When I found out she backed out I wasn't especially happy. I was scared. Can I handle it myself?

T: So you use the defenses of being passive, of not knowing, of acting inadequate, and then you can't see yourself as up to the job.

P: That's right.

T: What are you experiencing right now?
(*Patient appears upset.*)

P: Fear.

T: How are you experiencing me?

P: You're pushing.

T: How do you feel to me for doing that?

P: Unfriendly.

T: Unfriendly?

P: I sense it. I don't feel hostile, but quite unfriendly.

T: What would you like to do?

P: I'm trying to find an answer. Darn it. You're right. I'm trying to find a way out. I'm looking for something to explain away and push aside the thrust of your observation. With that frame I can't go anywhere. I don't know how my low self-esteem and my defense mechanisms go hand in hand.
(*Working alliance.*)

T: Do you feel I made you look bad?

P: Yes. I feel embarrassed.

T: I did something bad to you.

P: Yes, and I feel defensive, and am trying to find a way out. What can I do?

T: Is being helpless a passive way to make me lay off?

P: That hits home. (*Short silence.*) It's easier to say I should be more positive. I fail in confrontations with my colleagues. I need time to think about what you said. Say it again. (*Passivity.*)

T: What?

P: How my reaction ties in with not wanting to look bad or not wanting Ted or Len to look bad. If I am more positive and challenging, I might make them look bad. So I fall back on my tricks?

T: How does that sound to you?
(*Trying not to collude with the passivity.*)

P: Logical.

T: What's missing is your fear of their reaction to your challenge, like what you felt toward me last session.

P: That makes sense. That's a lot to think about.

Session 4

P: The more I think about the conclusion, I'm too afraid to rub people the wrong way, to make them look bad. That's one of the major handicaps to my moving ahead. For example, I and my wife are aware of it. We bend over backward trying to be nice and not rub people the wrong way. How can I change my attitude? It's a habit. I react without thinking and that puts me in a subservient position and I can't get out of it. For example, one of my colleagues left to go to a different project. My car was behind his car. I debated whether I wanted to wave at him or not. I'm guessing I was concerned that he might not like me if I didn't wave.

T: How were you feeling toward him at that moment?
(*Cutting through obsessive style.*)

P: Mixed. He's good and I'd like him on my project. But maybe I'm a little threatened.

T: The threat is the competition?

P: I have the premise that he's better than I am technically. The way he behaves. He says things with conviction.

T: How do you feel toward him then?

P: Uneasy.

T: Uneasy?

P: When people come on strong and I don't like it. When you talk about technical facts you're either right or wrong. But I'm uneasy.

T: So the issue is the coming on strong.

P: We were discussing Larry. If I decide someone is more knowledgeable, there's no problem listening.

T: But how do you feel to him about that?

P: I know he's good.

T: I ask the negative side and you go to the positive side. You said you felt threatened.
(*Confronting denial.*)

P: He may come in and take over things I'm doing. Then he'll look good in the eyes of the superiors. I won't look as good.

T: You act passive and he looks good.

P: I didn't do anything.

T: How did you feel to him then?

P: I tried to shut him off.

T: You didn't answer my question. You told me what you did.

P: You want to know how I felt?

T: Yes.

P: I shut off my emotions.

T: Are you doing that now?

P: I don't like him that much, but it would be nice if he could stay and help the project.

T: What are the negative feelings?

P: I don't like him too much.

T: What do you mean?

P: The times he comes on too strong.

T: Can you give me an example?

P: No. I don't like him at all. I act cold. I stop the conversation.

T: What would you like to do?

P: Now I'm feeling indoctrinated. I'd like to punch him in the nose.

T: You're saying that to please me?

P: Maybe. That's why I used the word indoctrinated. I keep quiet and act cool.

T: You use a passive way to express your anger.

P: I think so. But he picked up on it. Lately he's been acting in a more passive manner.

T: How do you feel about how he is now?

P: He's okay.

T: You dealt with the problem in a passive manner.

P: It's a habit I don't like. I don't know what to do about it.

T: You're being passive and helpless with me now. (*Interpreting resistance.*)

P: (*Laughs*) I want to do something about it.

T: Like what?

P: I don't know. I can say something more. My wife is very sensitive. If people rub her the wrong way she fights back and tells them she doesn't like it. She comes on too strong.

T: To you?

P: She used to, but not recently. Five years ago when she did that I felt the same way. I resented it, and then I withdrew. Now she's mellow. I bring this example as evidence of what I don't want to be.

T: You seem to equate getting ahead as an aggressive act.

P: Other colleagues are more aggressive and assertive and they got ahead. I tell myself I want to be assertive.

T: But the more angry you are the more you retreat.

P: Yes. I just thought that if I really want to express a point that would hurt the other or rub him the wrong way. I have to work myself up so I can be assertive or say something unpleasant to the other person. I don't like it. It drains me. I don't want to be always on guard and prepared. What do I want to do?

T: You said you wanted to get ahead. That seems clear.

P: Yes. Now I'm confused.

T: When did you get confused?

P: When you said that about moving ahead.

T: Do you know how?
(*Should have inquired how that statement created anxiety.*)

P: Not by punching in the nose.

T: Is that what you feel like doing?

P: Yes.

T: So you know you feel resentful but you smooth it over.

P: I could just tell them I don't like how they behave. That would be offensive.

T: What would happen then?

P: I'd take the other by surprise.

T: You'd hope they'd back down?

P: It's a dilemma. What if they're right? I don't want him to back down.

T: You said you would be offensive. How do you imagine he'd respond?

P: He might come back and be harsh. Maybe the thing to do is to stay calm and talk about the issue and leave emotions out of it. I seem to be drifting.

T: What are you experiencing?

P: Fear.

T: Toward me?

P: I'm not sure. I feel confusion.

T: The confusion acts like a smoke screen.

P: A mask. If someone comes on strong to me the only thing to say is that he is too strong and let's calm down and talk about the issue. It depends on the circumstances.
(*This probably refers to the transference.*)

T: Give me an example.

P: Larry. I'd tell him let's calmly sit down and talk about it. Instead I shut him off. I can't think of a social situation.

T: How about your wife?

P: I've conditioned her.

T: You said you had the same problem in the family.

P: Yes. I don't speak up. I can't recall an incident right now. A friend of ours told us she'd take care of something and backed down. I didn't say anything.

T: How did you feel toward her?

P: I would have liked to have said, "You said you would!" But I didn't. I hate myself for being that way.

T: You turn the anger on yourself.

P: Yes. I'm always like that. I try to say it in a vague way, and then I hate myself for not spelling it out.
(*On the way out.*) Is there any clue?
(*Retreat to passivity.*)

Session 5

P: I want to continue about Larry. He called me today and asked if he could come back to our project. Maybe I don't want it because I fear the competition. Before I wanted him to come back because I needed someone to lean on. I think I can deal with people I know better than with a stranger. My feelings about having him back are he's someone I need to lean on technically. But he might compete with me. Since I feel good about myself because I just had a few days off, I'm leaning toward forgetting about it. I don't feel so strong about having someone to lean on any more. That's a change from the feeling we talked about. I was thinking I may have reasons for why when the going gets rough I turn it back on myself. It has to do with my parents. They wanted me to do things the same way. Since I didn't, when I ran into a road block, the only way I could get

their attention was to act in meek self-pity, so they would give me sympathy and notice me. If I fought them I'd only get a scolding.
(*He begins to look at his defensive style.*)

T: There was gratification in it even if it didn't feel very good.

P: It occurs to me that it fits the picture. That's one thing about psychology — you can twist things.

T: Are you twisting things when you say it fits?

P: I don't know how much it is because I am biased.

T: Do you think I may know better?

P: No. No one knows better than I do because I am who I am, but I think I could be influenced. I try to make things fit the premise. It fits my behavior. I try to mold into a prominent personality or event.

T: And that's going on with me?

P: It could be.

T: Let's look at that.

P: It also fits. I tend to mold myself into the environment. I don't stand up and be different. I don't know. It's too easy to twist things.

T: Are you twisting to fit in with me?

P: Yes. To fit the premise we are building. I turn it back to myself rather than be aggressive and try to change the dominating factor.

T: Is there something you disagree with me about but haven't said? You give me a lot of power.

P: Yes, I do. Also with my colleagues. I don't like that I give myself up before a confrontation or interaction starts.

T: Then how do you feel toward that person?

P: Subversive. I mean subservient.

T: That's the same error you made before.

P: But I also want to knock you down and be the one who is one better.

T: So that's why you said subversive.

P: It fits.

T: You have wishes to knock me down.

P: Yes. I don't like to be bossed around. I feel helpless. I give you total authority and don't even struggle. I don't like it. I can link that to my parents.

T: You had a wish to knock them down.

P: It's too far back. The only emotion I have now is I have to oblige them grudgingly.

T: Grudgingly?

P: I feel disgusted with myself. I feel helpless because I couldn't do anything about it. They were my parents. They knew better.

T: Do you have a reaction to what you just said?

P: No. The only thing I felt was that I was forceful when I put myself in their shoes, but I don't feel my own feelings. I erase myself. That's the pattern.

T: You felt their power but not your own.

P: Yes.

T: To be powerful would be to knock them down, like here with me.

P: Not physically. But to gain the upper hand. At work today I was able to speak more confidently. I felt I had the upper hand. I can only handle things at two levels — either I have the upper hand and am in complete control or it's the other way around. I don't know how to be in between.

T: That seems to be the issue here.

P: And I do things to please you.

T: You make sure I don't feel threatened by you.

P: That's right. (*Sighs*)

T: What are you experiencing right now?

P: Speaking about threatening — it occurred to me this week when I was driving to work, I asked myself if we were trying to find out the underlying things in me. I wonder and thought I should ask you if I am getting anywhere. Am I getting my money's worth?

T: You're giving me the power to answer that.

P: This question would be aggressive to ask.

T: The form of the question is a subservient way to communicate.

P: That's true. It would take guts even to ask. Then I'm subservient.

T: What are the feelings and statement behind the question?

P: I'm looking for a prescription. When we know the problem there must be a prescription.

T: And I know it.

P: Yes.

T: That's what you did with Dr. L. You kept him knowing the answer and had to keep coming back to have your batteries recharged.
(*The unresolved transference.*)

P: I liked him, but I think you're right. I kept coming back for the prescription.

T: You kept yourself subservient to him and gave him all the power.
(*Transference resistance.*)

P: Is that true? It's a good time to try to merge the two things together. Dr. L. said that because of my parents' behavior to me, the premise was set up that I am inadequate, and that's the premise for all my behavior. I was brainwashed. It's consistent if I try to act and not rub them the wrong way that I become inadequate.

T: Your feelings of inadequacy are related to your passive defenses against your own impulses and wishes.
(*Upward interpretation of narcissistic issues.*)

P: It's true I needed Dr. L. to recharge. I drift back and need someone to shake me.

T: How come?

P: I'm used to it.

T: There's a point at which you don't like it and have to push your feelings away.

P: You say I have feelings or impulses to knock down and not be subservient.
(*The projection should be noted.*)

T: What are you doing now?

P: I'm confused.

T: You got confused when I took the upper hand.

P: And you put me on the defensive. When the other gets the upper hand, I ask questions instead of confronting. Back to my question. I can explain everything. So what?

T: You are being helpless.

P: I see. (*Laughs*) You're really throwing it back at me.

T: How does that make you feel?

P: I was feeling scared. There's something in that. Maybe I try to do things on an intellectual level and suppress my emotions. What does it mean? Maybe the intellectual garbage is an escape. I don't let my emotions show. It just occurred to me. I tie it in with my parents. When I felt bad or tried to knock them down, I suppressed it. I had to explain it away. They were my parents and I had to be respectful. I couldn't handle my emotions. Having to let my emotions show is one of the answers.

T: How does that thought make you feel?

P: A little scared.

T: What's the danger?

P: If I ask you something I take a risk. I may annoy you or rub you the wrong way. That's probably it.

T: Then what would happen?

P: I don't know. Now I feel like I'm acting to get sympathy. I was going to say I'm afraid you'll come back with bigger vengeance.

T: Then what?

P: I could fight back.

T: What would you do?

P: In a personal situation, if I know I'm right, I would try to do it in a mild manner.

T: How would you fight back in a mild manner?

P: I would hold on to my principles or ideas. I'd tell you as often as it takes. I'm thinking too far ahead. There's no end to it — two people talking to the wall. It wouldn't get the work done. I might bring in a new point, but if we were just emotional, we'd shout at each other.

T: How does that feel?

P: Scary.

T: What's the danger?

P: We'd come to blows.

T: What would happen?

P: I'd be knocked down or hurt.

T: Then what would you do?

P: I would keep fighting in my fantasy.

T: How do you feel about it?

P: They're just words.

T: How would you feel if you were knocked down?

P: I might kick or scream.

T: Where would you kick the person?
    (*This should have been related to the transference.*)

P: Where it hurts — where I could reach him. In my fantasy I would fight with whatever power I could.

T: How do you feel about your fantasy?

P: Nothing. Not even fear. Before, there was fear.

T: Before you thought about fighting back?

P: Yes. But nothing now.

T: Do you feel good about it?

P: No. Now the fear is back. It isn't good and it isn't bad. It's a territory I've never been in.

T: But you fear it in your mind.

P: Even in this fantasy I couldn't shake myself free from reality. I'm trying to placate you again, but there is the constraint of reality. He might be bigger. I might get hurt.

T: You're still staying away from feeling.

P: I have the idea now that I am trying to placate you. (*He begins to confront his resistance on his own.*)

Session 8

P: I had a direct conflict with Ted. I knew what was happening all along. I couldn't say the proper words.

T: What were the exact circumstances?
(*Asking for specifics.*)

P: There was a meeting with Ted and his bosses. A point was brought up by the people who are helping me with the project. They presented a list of things still to be done, both large and small things. Ted's bosses asked questions and dwelt on it. I sensed something wasn't right. After the meeting Ted asked me to get the solution to one of the points. The next day I talked with him and he blew up. He said it was a trivial point and he didn't want his bosses to waste time, as though we couldn't solve such a trivial problem. It makes us look bad. I was mad too.

T: About what?
(*Asking for clarification.*)

P: He seemed to blame me. It's not fair to blame me for that. I was also mad because at the meeting it seemed like the people who helped me stole the limelight. They got credit for my ideas. I didn't come out. I could have put it in the right perspective, given my ideas. But I didn't. It didn't occur to me but I knew I was mad that they were getting the glory. The next day I was mad that Ted was mad at me. I told him it was because we didn't want anything to fall between the cracks. He said we looked bad because it was trivial. I said it was a complete list and that we hadn't gotten around to doing it because it was low priority. I was mad at the people and at Ted.

T: Did you tell Ted you were mad?

P: No, but I think he knew it. His voice cracked and his face was red. Normally there's nothing I could do to Ted.

T: Like what?

P: Rebut him.

T: How do you feel about it right now?

P: More mad than anything else. Later I talked to my colleague and he said if Ted's bosses were interested, that's just the way it is. It hit me, that's what I should have told Ted. But I was blank. Now I see Ted's problem. If I came up with a cold rational statement, I would shut him off. You sense in me that I want to knock him down in one punch. I didn't pick the right punch. I ended up doing what he told me to do.

T: You used the word rebuttal. You said you were angry but your words were defensive.

P: An offensive stance didn't occur to me.

T: The feelings are angry, the words are placating and self-justifying. You changed being active to being passive.

P: I defended myself.

T: You did not challenge him.
   (*The passive stance toward the authority figure.*)

P: That's true. It didn't occur to me to say what my colleague said.

T: It didn't occur to you to challenge him, but just to placate him.

P: I defended myself. What else can I do?

T: You are being passive with me.

P: And you say what do I want to do. It doesn't even trigger anything in my head.

T: You are automatically self-defensive and passive.

P: I was in the meeting, too, with the people who helped me and got the credit. I'm mad at them, but I didn't challenge them.

T: What stops you?

P: Myself. That's being vague.
(*He catches his resistance.*)

T: Yes.

P: The fear I may displease the other party. They might come back and punish me, or give me a hard time.

T: What would you do then?

P: As I am, retreat. As I would like to be, fight back. But then, maybe that's just the indoctrination.

T: (*Shrugs*)

P: Deep down I want to fight back or I wouldn't be seeking help here. I shy away from the challenge. I'm insecure.

T: You retreat from aggression. You turn to defensive passivity.

P: The fact I realized I'm afraid to challenge because the other might give me a hard time doesn't erase or overcome it, but the realization is a first step. The next time maybe I'll realize I have an option or alternatives versus backing down and turning it on myself. That's the bottom line. Then it's up to me; I'd have a choice or option to make rather than just react. Act rather than react.
(*A shift toward readiness to working through.*)

T: How do you feel right now?

P: I feel good. It's something concrete to work on. It bugs me when things are vague and there's no specific direction. I feel good. Also scared. Something new just occurred to me. It just occurred that what I'm saying is

nothing new to the extent that Dr. L. said the same thing. This is a different version. He said I have the option to take action on the old premise of an inadequate me or a new premise that I feel good about myself. You said something about accepting the challenge. That's more specific. I did use Dr. L. as a crutch. What's the difference now?
(The competitive motivation was missed in his previous treatment.)

T: What is it?

P: Now I say it out loud in a conscious manner. Before subconsciously I knew I'd have to recharge.

T: In your relationship with him, you got permission to challenge. But even now you don't own your own aggression. You attribute it to my "indoctrination."

P: That is the point. Now I'm thinking what it means to own it. I probe the consequences. If I'm responsible for my own act or say it was someone else's idea. I just blanked out.
(Indicating resistance.)

T: What are you experiencing?

P: Scared. I'm scared.

T: Because you can't back down and say, "Don't be mad at me. It was Dr. L.'s idea or Dr. Horner's idea or my wife told me to do it."

P: That's right. That's one point that didn't hit me. I don't know what to say. It is the point. *(Silence)* I'm thinking that it's true. At home I hide behind my wife. At work I hide behind whoever is convenient. When I ask someone else to do a certain task, instead of saying I want him to do it, I use Ted's name or the name of some higher authority.

T: Mhm.

P: Why would I not want to own that it's my idea or action? If I did, I would sound more aggressive. I'd rub someone the wrong way.

T: (*Shrugs*)

P: Is there a connection between that and the fear of challenge?

T: When you ask me questions, you back down from a subtle challenge of my authority.
(*Interpreting passivity as resistance.*)

P: That's true. I can think of that scenario with my parents. The times I challenged them and they came back hard on me. To alleviate the situation, I'd disown the idea or the alternative of challenging them. It makes sense. They'd always negate whatever idea I had to challenge them. If I did challenge them, I'd say it was someone else's idea to smooth over the situation.

T: How do you feel toward them about having to do that?

P: I hate it!!
(*The first expression of strong affect.*)

T: You must hate it with me too.

P: (*Sighs*) Not yet.

T: You assume the defensive posture with me by asking questions.

P: That's true. But I'm confused. (*Laughs*) Confused. I treat this situation like you are the teacher and I'm going to school.

T: And you never challenged your teachers.

P: For sure. It was an extension of my attitude to my parents.

T: You keep yourself dumb and the teacher and me smart and knowing everything. That's a placating stance.

P: It definitely is, and at times I knew I was doing it on purpose to make the other party feel good, to placate, and I don't like it. (*Sighs*) I don't like it at all! (*Silence*) (*Laughs*)

T: What's going on?

P: I just have to go out and fight. That was a cynical laugh. Maybe self-pity. Why didn't I do that? (*Silence*) (*Sighs*)

Another thing that's interrelated. A lot of times challenging is not a way to get something done in the project. You have to coax the other, to get them to do something for you to get the job done. But it doesn't conflict
with the concept of challenge. You have to know what
you're doing, if that's the way to get the job done. It
has nothing to do with challenging. It all makes sense.
But it is easier said than done.
(*Working alliance.*)

T: There's always the alternative—don't do it and continue
to feel the way you feel.

P: That would be chicken. And I don't like it. Subconsciously I haven't shaken my own program, the way I
do things, but I do not like it!

Session 14

P: How have I been doing? I'm the one to answer that.

T: How come you asked me?

P: Maybe I experienced the need to recharge. I'm not
making a lot of progress in owning my own actions.

T: Last session we were starting to touch on family issues. Do you think you might want to pull away from
that subject?

P: I don't know. I want a better feeling of how we stand.
It's not going to be open-ended.

T: That's right. We agreed to a 40-session maximum. This
is number 14.

P: It's time we should see if we're going in the right direction.

T: Do you have any thoughts about this?

P: No. The first few sessions we were uncovering new material. Now it's stagnant.

T: What seems to be missing?

P: We're not moving.

T: What was your reaction to our last session?

P: No reaction. I always said there is a stretch of 10 to 12 years that I don't remember of early childhood. I suppress it. It must have some bearing.

T: What do you remember of the last session?

P: The fact that I couldn't deal with my uncle and hoped that my father would stand up to him for me. But he didn't. He let me down. The consequence is my habit of hiding behind someone I've put on a pedestal.

T: You've cut yourself off from your feelings about this. Maybe that's the piece that's missing.

P: I cut myself off because it's painful.

T: What are you experiencing right now?

P: I'm trying to reconstruct it. I recollect other clues of childhood.

T: Who was the dominant one, of your mother and father?

P: My mother. She was with us most of the time.

T: How was that?

P: I really couldn't care less, now. (*Denial.*)

T: How about then?

P: I was closer to my brother and sister than to them. My sister was three years older and my brother was three years younger.

T: Who took care of you?

P: My sister was on her own with her friends. My mother always complained to us that my aunt and uncle gave her a hard time. She asked us to study to make her look good.

T: How did you feel about that?

P: The feeling was I had to try to protect her and take care of her. That was the dominant feeling, not love.

T: What's the difference between feeling loving and protecting?

P: It was different in our family. We never showed feelings. With my mother and father it was business as usual. We all had a part to play.

T: You said you wanted to protect your mother.

P: Yes.

T: It sounds like there were feelings there.

P: I felt she was stepped on, and she couldn't defend herself.

T: Who stepped on her?

P: My uncle.

T: How did you feel toward him for stepping on your mother?

P: Mad. I hated him. It was all I could do — hate. I couldn't do anything. At times I'd blow up and dispute him. I'd say something to his face, and then my mother would be the first to come down on me. It wasn't proper. It would incur more punishment on her. They'd say she didn't raise us properly to respect him and all that crap.

T: You felt loving and protecting to your mother, but you didn't get any loving appreciation back.

P: That's true.

T: How does that feel — to try to protect her and not to be rewarded with her love?

P: Betrayed! I stand up for you and you let me down! Betrayed. She might have explained afterwards and I might or might not have understood, but the immediate feeling was that I was betrayed. After awhile I closed my eyes and ears and said the hell with it.
   (*Strong affect.*)

T: It sounds like there was a wish to be specially loved by your mother.

P: I think so. By comparison my father lacks feeling, though mother plays her part. I interacted with her more, and feelings developed more with her. My father was away at work. I didn't see him much. There wasn't any communication.

(The wish to be preferred by father over his brother came out in an earlier session.)

T: Did your mother complain to you about your father?

P: No. The complication was that although I had love for my mother, because of her lack of love for my father, she was always nagging. We were the only ones she could hold on to as hers. It was the negative component of my feelings to her. In my relationship with her now, she tells me to take care of myself and the kids, nagging. I act like them to my kids.

T: You want your son to make you look good the same way.

P: Yes.

T: So there was a triangle with you and your mother and your uncle. You wanted to be special to her, but he'd win out and be more important to her.

P: I see. And my father was always on my uncle's side. There was no one to turn to. That's why I gave up.

T: You couldn't challenge your uncle's power and get specially loved by your mother for it, and you were mad at your father for not helping against your uncle.

P: Yes. I'm trying to think how this ties in with how I am now. It's obvious. I did try to challenge the authority, but I got back doom. In the family, everyone put me down, including the ones I hoped would back me up. Now it's a habit not to challenge. I expect the consequence of failure.

T: Last time you were saying how you did challenge Ted and won, but you didn't like that either, because then you couldn't keep him on a pedestal. You want him to be strong to stand up for you.

P: In the same context I talked with Marion. She was saying how she'd do things and I disagreed. She said she has 18 years of experience. I didn't say anything.

T: How did you feel?

P: I thought, baloney! So what! I still believed what I said.

T: She's like the uncle who can't be challenged?

P: Yes. That's a good point. Someone else came and she turned to talk to him. I didn't feel too bad about that. It did bother me a little bit.

T: A little bit?

P: It bothered me.

T: You turned it on yourself, then you made it small, like you had to respect your elders.

P: I don't have to be bothered.

T: You push it away as you did in your family. It's obvious you are bothered.
(*Cutting through the denial.*)

P: I *am* bothered by it.

T: Let's take a look at that.

P: The reason I am bothered is I believe what I said and then I was challenged by the authority.

T: You were diminished, as a child. She has 18 years of experience.

P: Now I'm feeling scared.

T: What's that about?

P: Fear.

T: What comes to mind?

P: Nothing. I'm blank.

T: Are you feeling fear toward me?

P: No. If anything, I'd like to get the fear out and talk with you.

T: You weren't afraid of Marion but you were of your uncle. How do you feel to the one who makes you feel afraid?

P: I don't like it.

T: That sounds angry. As I push you, you get frightened.

P: Yes.

T: Maybe you are afraid of your own anger.

P: I don't remember where I expressed anger and didn't get bad consequences.

T: You got mother's betrayal.

P: That's right. It's interesting. I still don't want to own it.

T: Betrayal is a harsh word.

P: Yes, that's how I felt.

T: Can you connect now with how that betrayal felt?

P: No. All I feel now is fear. Scared. In here (*pointing to his chest*). I feel empty. A numbness.

T: Maybe the emptiness is the loss of your mother's love. You started by trying to be specially loved by her and then you lost that love.

P: Yes. I don't know what to think.

T: What are you feeling?

P: The same, but not as much. I hear what you said and I understand it.

T: Does that make you sad?

P: I feel lost. Maybe that's also a defense mechanism. I don't feel sad. That confuses the issue. I feel lost and I want someone to help.
(*These are undoubtedly preoedipal issues. They are not picked up.*)

T: Mhm.

P: I have an interesting blank in my head. (*Silence*) I can tell myself that if I challenge the authority now, nothing will happen to my mother. Marion has influence on Ted, and I don't want to rub her the wrong way. I don't like her as a person. She's too domineering.

T: That's what you said about your mother.

P: That's true. In a way my wife could also be called domineering, hot-headed. She does things her way. I'm probably more attached to people who dominate than not.

T: And you have to find a way to be special to that person. With your wife, you are protective with her about her work. You play out the same theme at work, wanting to be special and afraid to challenge.

P: I don't want to be a slave to the past.

Session 16

P: I ran into Ted this morning. He had to cancel a meeting because he had to take his car in for repair. I asked him if he needed a ride. On the way back, I didn't say much. Then I said I'd take him back to pick up his car. I'm so ready to offer help. I don't know if it's just a habit of trying to please, or am I playing politics.

T: We've talked about your wish to be special to your father over your brother and to be special to your mother over your uncle. Is there a wish to be special with Ted?

P: There definitely is. I want to be special with the boss.

T: It seems to have the same emotional meaning as being special to your mother and father.

P: Yes. I want to know what I'm doing and why. If I don't think about it the chances are I'll act on the old stuff. I want to catch it before I react. I want to act, not react.

T: The wish to be special leads to placating behavior, though you wonder if it's political.

P: I always have a placating attitude. Speaking of that, a lot of times I tend to find a reason why I should want to, why I should be obligated to. I look for something in which he did me a favor and I am obligated.

T: Obligated to be nice?

P: Like the time our friend got us that special deal.

T: Do you think you may project that if you do someone a favor then you expect to be treated nicely—to be specially loved?

(Connection to the wish to be special to his mother for

doing her a favor, that is, standing up to the uncle,
should have been made.)

P: What's wrong with that?

T: You said it was a problem.
(*Confronting the denial.*)

P: I try to find the good intention no matter how evil the
person is. I look for the shred of goodness and try to
protect it. I justify why they do that.

T: What could be behind that?

P: It dictates how I behave. My concern is whether I do
it because of my good nature or for political reasons.
I look for any good intention in the other.

T: How about your parents?

P: That's what I was thinking, that I try to deceive myself.
I don't want to think that my parents could ignore me
and not appreciate what I've done for them. I try to
justify for them and make excuses.

T: How would you feel if you didn't make excuses for
them?

P: Rejected.

T: How do you feel to someone who rejects you?

P: Angry. Mad. I wanted to love my parents. I don't want
to admit that they rejected me, so I justify them.
(*Defense against ambivalence.*)

T: You explained away what they did to make you angry.

P: Right. (*Silence*) That makes sense.

T: What are you experiencing?

P: A little scared. An empty feeling. I'm not sure if empty
is the right word. It's congested. Tight.

T: Do you feel like crying?

P: Not so much. It's more fear. I don't cry when I'm scared.
I do when I'm sad.

T: A minute ago when you said you felt congested, you
hit your hand with your fist.

P: I did? (*Silence*)

T: Does feeling scared have to do with your anger?

P: I'm back to feeling scared because I'm afraid that my anger could be very destructive. I'm not sure I understand this. The destructiveness. People won't love me any more. It's all a house of cards. Being a nice guy and being well loved — it would all collapse. (*Sighs*) I don't know what to say.

T: What are you experiencing?

P: An emptiness in my head.
(*Again, the preoedipal issues are not picked up.*)

T: How does all this relate to what you were saying about Ted?
(*Returning to the focal conflict.*)

P: I said earlier that I want to see whether I did that for political reasons or because of the habit of being "Mr. Nice Guy." I want to be Mr. Nice Guy, because I try to get the shred of goodness from anyone. It's my reaction to my parents' reaction. It's the same with Ted. I did say Marion is now his favorite. Because of that, I feel competitive to get his attention. It is possible this may be a consequence of that. I feel Ted rejects me. I'm confused. So I want to please him to get his attention. I show him the shred of goodness in me so I can be of use to him.

T: Emotionally it's like competing with your uncle for your mother and with your brother for your father.

P: It's a no-win situation. I would have made the offer even if Marion were not in the picture. It's a habit to do something to please my parents because I felt their rejection when I stood up for them. Other times I show I can be a nice boy and of use for them. With Ted, it's the same reason even if Marion were not there. The ultimate goal is the same. To show the shred of goodness and usefulness in me to the authority figure. The bottom line is I have to convince myself I'm good just by standing on my own feet.

T: That one can do by doing a job well. You make it a personal issue with emotional meaning.

P: That's right. You say I mix something personal in the work environment.

T: Yes. That's why there is so much uncertainty and anxiety about it.
(*Interpreting transference issues in the work context.*)

P: This time I want to look into it. I must be anxious or I would not have brought it up. In a sense, I don't even care if Ted likes me. Before when we drove together I'd initiate conversation and make it pleasant. Now I don't care. I was cryptic. I just discussed work or professional things. That's an improvement. But there's still the same anxiety. That reminds me. We were on the topic of my wife last time.

T: How do the things we are talking about now apply there?

P: Sometimes she does things to irritate me a lot because of her sloppiness. The kids take after her. I'm mad about it. I used to pick up for her, but I gave up.

T: Is that all you did?

P: No. I told her the place was like a pig pen. She joked about it. Sometimes she picks up and sometimes she doesn't. She complains there's too much to do. She hides behind that and says there are more important things.

T: What does sloppiness mean to you?

P: (*Laughs*) I could tie it to this fact. One way I tried to please my mother was to be tidy. She liked things tidy, everything in its place. It's something I still follow because I wanted to please her.

T: The wish to please her and to be special is very strong.

P: It seems to be. I wasn't aware of that. I can explain many things in that context. I'm also thinking about wanting my kids to be good in school. I wanted a reflection from them.

T: To look good.

P: Yes, but I wonder if it can't be explained because I wanted to please my mother.

T: If you look good, it pleases her because then she looks good.

P: It's so strong. I just want to be myself.

T: First you have to be aware of the unconscious factors that direct what you do. The wish to please your mother is very powerful.

P: It sure is. It sure is. And it's scary too.

Session 17

P: Last time I realized what a tremendous influence my mother still has on me. It's related to my inhibition in challenging an authority. When I did, what I got back was an unpleasant experience. I got a twisted way of looking at the experience and tried to explain away my mother's behavior. We were talking about incidents when I was mad at my wife. She usually goes to sleep with the TV on. The other day she was in bed and I went in and turned it on. She was mad and said I disturbed her sleep. I was really mad. I turned it off and left the room. I thought, how could I know, especially when it's her habit to leave it on. I went into the study and said, "Damn it!" I don't know if she heard me, but later when I went back to our room she apologized. She knew she had been unreasonable. That kind of thing happens a lot. She blows up and jumps to conclusions. Sometimes she's right and sometimes she's wrong, but I've always had to take it. I either talk to her about it or ignore it.

T: So the "Damn it!" was different.

P: Yes. It's new to me to let it out. I still don't know how to handle it.

T: Let's look at your relationship with her in more detail.

P: To me I do what I do best—I take care of her. I anticipate her needs and try to make things smooth and easy for her. That's how I show affection.

T: How are things with your sex life together?

P: Adequate. She doesn't like it. There's an inhibition in her, but she goes along with me.

T: What's that like for you?

P: Sometimes alright. At times I say, "The hell with it. It's more trouble than I wanted." She's aware of it and does on occasion try to smooth things over.

T: Is it a source of tension?

P: I think it is. Sometimes I want sex and she says no. I was going to say I don't think I'm unreasonable, asking too much. We used to talk about it. From our cultural background sex is dirty. She still has that idea, so I understand.

T: How was it growing up? What did you see or hear?

P: It was always taboo. No one talked about it. It was the culture.

T: How did young people learn about it?

P: Through rumors. When a girl gets married her mother talks to her. That would be it. In our culture it's something you do in private. You don't talk about it. My wife's exposure was minimal.

T: What about your own?

P: In college I went to see X-movies with friends.

T: What was that like for you?

P: It was exciting, titillating. I like to watch it when I get mad.

T: When you get mad?

P: Yes. Sex is a way of getting back at the woman.

T: You use it against your wife?

P: Not consciously, but I wouldn't be surprised if I did.

It's a way to get even. It might not be out of reason to say possibly I do it to get back at my mother. It's a symbolic form of aggression.

T: What are you getting back at her for?

P: Maybe the oppression I got from her. I talked to my uncle and she let me down. Maybe that's stretching it.

T: Do you think your wish to be special had sexual overtones?

P: It never occurred to me. My thinking could be influenced by reading today why a madman behaves as he does. There might be that connection, but as far as I know, not.
(*This should have been taken further.*)

T: So by oppression you mean your mother dominated you, and this is a way to dominate the woman?

P: I suppose so. Maybe this is something my wife doesn't like.

T: What is that?

P: My attitude. I don't think so, but it didn't help. In the beginning she didn't like sex at all and provoked anger in me and triggered my reaction to want to get back at my mother. It made things worse. I have tried to make it easier and pleasant for her, but it doesn't help.

T: You were frustrated by both your mother and your wife.

P: To some extent. It's something that would reinforce bottling up my emotion. I know my wife tries. It's hard to know what I can say or do. (*Silence — sigh*) I do feel my sex life is okay. It's not the best, but it could be worse. Maybe I'm trying to explain it away, but I think I can handle it. My feeling inhibited goes much deeper and goes back to my mother. The way my wife is doesn't help. I appreciate that she really cares for me and the kids. That's the most important thing in a marriage. At times it does irk me that she doesn't want it.

T: The other evening when you went into the bedroom and

turned on the TV, were you wishing she'd be available for sex that night?

P: I don't remember. She's been under a lot of pressure at work and has been having trouble sleeping so I tend not to raise the issue. Our normal habit is to turn on the TV, on occasions with the kids. Her attitude is let them enjoy life and don't push. Before we got married she was very popular and I was kind of a loner. Now I have more professional friends. This week Ted and Marion and I were on a business trip and had to stay overnight. I was conscious of trying to control what I did. The principles I held to were to be myself and I made my opinions known, like where I wanted to eat. Then I'd say what they wanted was okay. Still I had some feeling of triumph that I was doing my thing.

T: How was it to be in the triangle with Marion closer to Ted?

P: I accepted the fact. It doesn't bother me. A lot of times I go out of my way to ask for her opinion. I was aware that Ted asked her if it was too windy when she sat in the back, but he didn't ask me. They went dancing that night. I did my own thing and called my wife. I felt on my own and in control of my own destiny. I felt well prepared for the situation.

T: You were working through what we've been talking about.

P: Yes. I think about it and what triggers what. If an event happened out of the blue, I might go back to my old way. It'll take time to change. I do feel I've begun to exert more, to take things under control at work. For one special task I've begun to bug management more for things I want, rather than passively just taking what I can get. I'm going into untested territory. I wonder how it would feel if I got bad feedback.

T: Will someone be like mother and give a negative reaction rather than a positive one?

P: Yes. I have to go through it and build up experience.

I'm trying to think about my overall relationship with my family, my colleagues, everybody. When things go okay, it's hard to isolate the problem areas.

T: Do you feel any different here with me?

P: I feel more comfortable with you. (*Laughs*) I don't know what to say. Comfortable is a vague word. Do you see any difference?

T: (*Smiling*) You ask fewer questions.
   (*This should have been a more direct interpretation of his once again deferring to the authority of the therapist.*)

P: I'm not trying to pass the buck. I feel more sure of myself. The fact that I suggest this different scenario or hypothesis and get positive feedback is encouraging. When you made the comment about my not asking questions, I felt some fear. It's still there, but it's out in the open. I can hardly wait for the time when it's not there.

T: You're still not sure if I'll be like your uncle or your mother and be angry.

P: Like the time I was able to say "Damn it" with my wife. It's a start. I want to be able to say it to someone's face, to say what my feeling is.

Session 25

In the 25th session the patient began to report changes that indicate a move toward termination.

P: I handle Marion better these days. I treat her as an equal. She and Ted and I had a meeting yesterday. She was defensive when I was presenting. I was monitoring my feelings in the meeting and noted that I was uptight at the beginning. After awhile I calmed down and then was able to carry on a conversation with Ted. He'd point out something and I could make a point or argue. It used to be all one way. He'd talk to me or I'd talk to him. Now there's some feedback. I was even able to smile a couple of times. Maybe Ted's used to my old behavior or it's his problem, but he seems uptight with me. Before he treated others more casually and me like he's the boss and is telling me what to do. That's how I treated myself.

T: And now you are different with him.

P: I calmed myself down. I wasn't defensive. I wasn't submissive.

T: You were willing to challenge his authority.

P: (*Later in session*) Lately I treat Marion more as an equal, and I'm not as concerned with pleasing or placating her. It all ties in together. In the last week or two I've tended to be more critical of people. I'm more outspoken if someone is not doing what I feel is necessary for getting the job done. . . . I would like to comment that when I feel good I feel a lot of people respect me more.

T: Mhm.

P: That should be obvious.

T: There's a tradeoff: being specially liked or loved is exchanged for being respected as an adult.

P: I talked with my father on the phone last week. I was more blunt with him . . . not as defensive. I told him what I felt. . . . Lately I'm making more decisions on my own without worrying how my wife feels about it. (*She recently told him she felt he was nicer to her.*)

T: They are all tied together.

P: I'm reliving through them but with a different premise and perspective.

Session 26

In this session we see the emergence of two resistances to ending treatment with the introduction of the loss issue, which came up two weeks earlier around fears that something might happen to his wife when she went on a trip alone, and the resurgence of the wish to preserve the authority figure qua authority. The positive transference necessary to the working alliance has always been manifest. We now see it as a resistance that must be dealt with quickly. Note the relevance of the opening remarks (the adaptive context).

P: I was thinking about why I was afraid to have my wife go to Washington without me. I think it's because I'm afraid of losing someone I love. As a kid I loved my parents and they let me down. I lost them.

T: Because you were angry about that?

P: Because I stood up. They turned against me. The experience of losing someone I loved was traumatic. That's why I'm so apprehensive now.

T: The wish for your parents is still there.

P: Oh yes. It's something I want to get rid of. I want them to love me, but I don't want it to be such a burden on me.

T: You turned the angry feelings of being betrayed on yourself to keep them good, to justify them.

P: That's why in any situation, if it doesn't go as I want, I tend to blame myself.

T: You've had to be good boy, good student, good employee, and good patient to be specially liked as you wanted to be.

P: Yes, so I waste a lot of energy trying to be the "good boy," whatever it is. . . . I haven't yet had a chance to be relieved of constraint to see if it would be any different.

T: Last time you were saying how it is different with Ted and Marion.

P: That's true. (*laughs*) Maybe I'm afraid if I take the credit for it I will offend someone. You're right.

T: If there is a change in you, it becomes a competition who gets the credit, you or I.

P: I consciously don't care how I get there.

T: If I get the credit, you'll still be dependent on me to recharge your batteries, as you were with Dr. L.

P: That is true.

T: Are you concerned how I will respond if you take the credit?

P: That didn't occur to me.

T: Not consciously. How does it sound right now?

P: If I start taking credit, I don't see how I take credit — if I notice improvement and said *I* did it?

T: Mhm.

P: It just occurred to me — I feel you'd be offended. Rather than look at the problem about who takes the credit, I shift to how you feel if I do such and such. You might be offended if I take the credit. I don't look at the question but am more concerned how people look at me.

T: How *I* look at you.

P: Right. This habit of being more afraid of offending people rather than getting into the problem and what to do about it.

T: If I am offended I might not like you.
(*T. should have added: and you might lose me as you lost your parents for standing up to them.*)

P: I might know inside that I take the credit.

T: You would have that secret, but you'd still be stuck interpersonally.

P: I felt I could manipulate Dr. L. I hid the secret in me.

T: You felt good inside, but you still felt stuck with him.

P: Yes, but that isn't the case here. I'm more open and on the level with you. So far as who takes the credit, we both have credit. I'm doing the inspection and you provide the clue where and how to look. But I feel it's something I have to do myself, not something you prescribe and I swallow it.

T: Mhm.

P: That's one of my anxieties — I still hope you have that pill.

T: If you could retreat to a more passive way you'd be less anxious.

P: Yes. It's hard to get rid of the constraints. It's partially due to my training. In technical training you work out a solution, and if it works, it's fine. Here there is an undoing of things that have been built up for over 40 years. I mix up my wishes with my anxieties. I wonder if what I just said was trying to placate.

T: Why would you do that now?

P: Maybe deep down I still think that if I take the credit you will be offended.

T: At the beginning of our session today you were talking about losing people who are important to you. Do you think that that concern about losing me would have to do with why you would placate now? After all, if you do well and can take the credit, our work will come to an end.
   (*T. should have added, "And that might feel like the same kind of loss you experienced with your parents."*)

P: That's entirely possible. You're the only one I can talk to and on an equal level without worrying about the consequences. So I like our relationship. On the other hand, I have a strong desire to be on my own two feet and get rid of the burdens that might hold me back. Right now I'm talking on an intellectual level, though there is a little scared feeling. This is the kind of conversation I would like to be able to have with my wife. I do feel this kind of situation is free of constraints and I'd like to work on it at work. The question is how to do it. (*laughs*) Now I'm getting back into the prescription business.

Bringing the positive transference, which was becoming a resistance, into awareness enabled the patient to relocate the wish appropriately in the relationship with his wife. With a resolution of the fear of offending the therapist, the patient was able to take his full share of the credit for the improvements that resulted from treatment and thus to become his own source of "power." This time there would be no need to return to the therapist to have his "batteries recharged."

Chapter 12

OUTCOMES

ISABEL SKLAR, M.S.W.

The efficacy of psychotherapy in general has been well documented in the literature. Research on specific types of treatment for specific types of diagnostic groups has been a more recent development. Malan (1963, 1976) and Davanloo (1978, 1980) have done considerable research into the outcome of short-term dynamic psychotherapy with patients suffering from various neurotic conditions.

The Importance of Transference/Parent Interpretations

In Malan's work (1976), the significant correlates with outcome were as follows: (1) motivation for insight on the part of the patient, (2) the focality of the treatment, i.e., the degree to which therapy was focused on a single theme, and (3) the transference/parent connection. The most significant factor in the determination of positive outcome was the number of transference/parent interpretations that was given in the course of the treatment. Malan developed the concept of a "transference/parent ratio." This was defined as the number of transference interpretations to the total number of interpretations recorded for each session. The higher the ratio, the more positive the treatment outcome. The quantity of these interpretations is important as it is indicative of the working-through process.

This concept, that successful outcome is highly correlated with the quantity and quality of transference/parent interpretations, is a major underpinning of psychoanalytic treatment. Malan and Davanloo have evidence that these kinds of interpretations are the major factor in the success of short-term treatment. Davanloo (1978) has reported that the more frequently these kinds of interpretations are given early in the treatment, the shorter the therapy will be.

Measurement of Outcome

For purposes of this book, outcome was measured through follow-up evaluations on patients that were discussed in previous chapters. Video-taped follow-up interviews, when possible, were done by an outside evaluator who was familiar with the patient's treatment, having seen at least the initial evaluation and having talked with the therapist. Though Malan's correlates were not used in this follow-up study, the clinical evidence is indicative of good therapeutic results.

Case Study: Sandra G.

The patient is a married woman in her thirties who suffered from panic attacks for a number of years prior to treatment. She connected the experience of palpitations and tachycardia to an ectopic pregnancy she had five years prior to treatment. They became worse in subsequent years, which included her ruminating and experiencing the fear of dying from a heart attack. She was placed on propranolol hydrochloride (Inderal) which decreased the frequency and intensity of these attacks. In the course of the evaluation, the patient's anxiety was connected to the request from her husband a few years earlier that she care for his mother, who was ill. This request had activated her own oedipal conflicts, as she was again put in the position of sharing a man with another woman. This also activated her unconscious death wishes for her mother. This oedipal configuration was a major aspect of the contract established for the treatment.

At intake the patient also described a conflictual relationship with both her parents. Her contacts with them were out of obligation, and her negative feelings toward them were kept in check, but were just below the surface.

Before treatment the patient complained of frequent bouts of depression where she would feel that everything was a burden and would have difficulty enjoying her life. All of these issues were connected to her oedipal problem and were addressed in the treatment.

The treatment lasted 22 sessions. At the time of termination she was entirely free of palpitations and discontinued propranolol. She expressed satisfaction about resolving important issues with her parents. Her overall adjustment at work, as well as with her husband, was quite satisfactory.

At follow-up, approximately 18 months after treatment, the patient continued to report an improvement in all her initial areas of disturbance. She had had two episodes of anxiety subsequent to the therapy, both of which had occurred under extremely stressful situations. One was on the death of her grandfather and the other was at the moment of adopting her son. Her relationship with her parents was considerably better; she no longer felt an obligation in her visits with them and enjoyed seeing them and sharing her life. She was less frequently depressed. Her decision to adopt a child was reflective of her improved outlook on life and the resolution of some major issues in the treatment. From all evidence, the patient sustained and continued to experience improvement in her feelings about herself and in her life subsequent to termination of treatment.

Case Study: Andrew B.

The patient, Andrew B., is a 35-year-old married man whose major complaint at intake was his inability to live up to his potential at work. He was unable to complete his course work at the university, and his doctoral dissertation remained unfinished. He complained of performance anxiety and also had difficulty in completing research on a project that he was involved with.

He also expressed anxiety about becoming a parent. He had

been fearful that he would become a father like his own father and was dreading the possibility of having a child. He also experienced severe difficulty in his relationships with men and with women. He remained distant and did not have any close relationships.

Early in the treatment the patient's oedipal conflicts were clarified. His close feelings for his mother and his strong competitive feelings for his father were brought into focus and became the work of the therapy. This conflict was connected to his areas of disturbance. At termination the patient was displeased with the treatment ending and expressed a wish to continue the work. He felt that his aggressive feelings were not sufficiently discussed in the treatment and that this was still a difficult area for him.

In the outcome evaluation, approximately 18 months after termination, the patient reported some changes in his initial areas of disturbance. His work situation remained basically unimproved. However, he did admit to a great improvement in his feelings about being a parent. Subsequent to the treatment he opened up a great deal in this area and was able to experience affection for his two children. He connected this to the treatment and his being made aware more of his positive feelings for his mother as well as putting into perspective the negative feelings he felt for his father. Though his feelings about himself as a parent were not as clear at termination, they were in evidence clearly at the outcome evaluation.

Case Study: Leo C.

This patient is a highly successful business man in his early fifties. He came to treatment with a presenting problem of free-floating and situational anxiety of four years' duration. In the evaluation he reported early memories of a close relationship with his mother and feelings that this was lost when he was about 5 or 6 years old. He also recalled a feeling of jealousy about his mother's preference for his father and remembers his father as a tough man with whom relationships were filled with anxiety. In the course of the evaluation, the connection between his current performance anxiety and the problems in the relationship with his father was made. The problem was viewed in this way, and the patient agreed to focus on this in treatment.

At follow-up two years posttreatment, the patient reported a considerable change in his areas of disturbance. His first problem, one of performance anxiety, had markedly improved. In fact, he had appeared recently on a news program on television and was able to perform extremely well. The second problem, relationship with his father, also was notably improved. He reported feeling a great deal of warmth from his father as a result of the change that took place as a result of treatment.

Case Study: Larry G.

This patient is a 30-year-old single man who came to treatment for an episode of depression relating to the ending of a relationship with a girlfriend with whom he had established a passive, dependent relationship. History revealed the patient had a warm, close relationship with his mother and a distant relationship with his father, as well as very competitive relationships with his siblings. In the initial evaluation the patient's sadness at the ending of his relationship with his girlfriend was connected to intense early attachments to his mother and his distancing from his father. This, then, became the focus of treatment.

At follow-up the patient reported an improvement in many areas of his life. He still suffered from depression, although it was considerably less significant than at the time he came for treatment. His relationship with his girlfriend was better than it had been, although there was still room for improvement. In relationship to his work, he felt very good. He had been working steadily and planned to complete his college education. He also reported a major improvement in his relationship with his parents. He gets along well with his father and feels relaxed with him. He has also been able to be assertive in his relationship with his mother and in general there is marked improvement in these areas. The patient also notices considerable improvement in his feelings about himself.

In summary, the clinical evidence indicates that patients show a marked improvement in short-term dynamic psychotherapy. The improvement has been sustained in follow-up of at least two years' duration. Though patients with simple oedipal conflicts seem to have the greatest success in treatment, patients with more severe psychopathology, including loss foci, also can benefit greatly from short-term dynamic psychotherapy.

References

Davanloo, H. (ed.) (1980). *Short-Term Dynamic Psychotherapy.* New York: Jason Aronson.

_____(1978). *Basic Principles and Techniques in Short-Term Dynamic Psychotherapy.* New York: SP Medical and Scientific Books.

Malan, D. (1963). *A Study of Brief Psychotherapy.* New York: Plenum Press.

_____(1976). *Towards the Validation of Dynamic Psychotherapy.* New York: Plenum Press.

APPENDIX

Table 2. Overall Ego Functioning Rating Scale
to Aid in the Selection of Candidates for STAPP
(Excellent, Good, Fair, Poor, Fail)

Relation to Reality

Good reality testing:	Patient can distinguish between wishes/fears and reality ( )
Sense of self as real:	Allowing for defensive depersonalization, patient experiences himself as real most of the time ( )
Can look at self objectively:	Patient can stand back and ally himself with the interviewer to explore patient's wishes, feelings, beliefs, actions ( )

Regulation and Control of Instinctual Drives

Capacity for delay:	Patient adapts readily to the delays of the intake process and can tolerate frustrations of wishes ( )
Adequate impulse control:	Patient can talk about sexual or aggressive impulses without having to discharge them into action ( )
Capacity for adaptive expression:	Control of sexual and aggressive impulses is not too rigid to allow for their appropriate expression in reality ( )

(continued)

Table 2. (*continued*)

Object Relations

Basic trust: Patient sees at least one person as benign and
                        trustworthy (   )

Relatedness: Patient is emotionally present and interper-
                        sonally engaged during the interview (   )

Differentiation: Patient is able to perceive interviewer and others
                        as separate and different from himself (   )

Stability: Patient can work with transference interpre-
                        tation without losing a realistic perception of
                        the interviewer (   )

Integration: Patient can tolerate ambivalence toward him-
                        self and others (   )

Maturity: Patient has been able to establish and maintain
                        true peer relationships (   )
                        Patient has history of altruistic relationship
                        (   )

Thought Processes

Patient can think conceptually and logically (   )

Defenses

Adequacy: Patient can tolerate negative and positive af-
                        fect (anxiety, depression, guilt, shame, anger,
                        love, affection, pleasure (   )
                        Patient can talk about negative and positive
                        affects (   )
                        Patient can recover readily from a regressive
                        reaction and talk about it (   )

Flexibility: Flexibility of defenses allows for their exami-
                        nation in the interview (   )

Maturity: Major defenses used are more advanced ones
                        of intellectualization, sublimation, repression,
                        rationalization or displacement without sig-
                        nificant recourse to more primitive modes of
                        projection, externalization, somatization, de-
                        nial, or introjection (   )

Table 2. (*continued*)

Autonomous Functions

Relative independence from conflict:	Speech, cognition, perception, motor behavior are not impaired in life or in the interview because of psychological reasons ( )
Recoverability:	If these functions are partially impaired, this can be understood and worked with in a psychological context by the patient ( )
Organic integrity:	There are no neurological disorders that would cause impairment that interfered with the ability to do the work of the interview ( )

Synthetic Function

Psychological mindedness:	Patient was able to think in terms of psychological cause and effect ( )
Capacity for insight:	Patient was able to draw valid psychological conclusions with respect to his own feelings, wishes, thoughts, and behavior ( )

Conscience

Standards of right and wrong:	Patient wants to live according to established standards of right and wrong ( )
Capacity for guilt:	Patient experiences guilt when he fails to meet these standards ( )
Realistic:	Standards do not require unrealistic perfection of morality ( )

Ego-Ideal

Feelings of worth:	Patient has well-established sense of self as a worthwhile person ( )
Realistic:	Patient image of self does not require unrealistic perfection or reveal grandiosity ( )

ADDITIONAL READINGS

Bruch, H. (1974). *Learning Psychotherapy*. Cambridge: Harvard University Press.

Colby, K. M. (1951). *A Primer for Psychotherapists*. New York: Ronald Press.

Freud, S. (1917). General theory of the neurosis: transference. *Standard Edition* 16:431–447.

Kernberg, O. (1975). *Borderline Conditions and Pathological Narcissism*. New York: Jason Aronson.

_____(1976). *Object Relations Theory and Clinical Psychoanalysis*. New York: Jason Aronson.

_____(1980). *Internal World and External Reality: Object Relations Theory Applied*. New York: Jason Aronson.

Kohut, H. (1971). *The Analysis of the Self*. New York: International Universities Press.

_____(1977). *The Restoration of the Self*. New York: International Universities Press.

Langs, R. J. (1973–74). *The Technique of Psychoanalytic Psychotherapy*. New York: Jason Aronson.

Mann, J., and Goldman, R. (1982). *A Casebook in Time-Limited Psychotherapy*. New York: McGraw-Hill.

INDEX